Ian Williams was born at Weymouth in Dorset and grew up on the coast. He studied at York University and spent the summer vacations working on the Isle of Wight. After graduating with a B.A. in 1976, he moved to the island permanently. With his brother he set up Wight Water, a windsurfing and watersports centre at Lake. He has been married for 22 years to Jill, who taught him to windsurf and tolerates his long sessions staring at a computer screen. He is co-author of five local guide booklets on cycling and walking.

Following page: Yachts at Yarmouth.

Diamond Coast

The Story of the Isle of Wight's Coast

IAN WILLIAMS

THE DOVECOTE PRESS

I dedicate this book to my father, whose love of books rubbed off on
me, and to my mother, who so eagerly awaited it
but will never see it.

First published in 2004 by
The Dovecote Press Ltd
Stanbridge, Wimborne, Dorset BH21 4JD

ISBN 1 904349 15 3

© Ian Williams 2004

Ian Williams has asserted his rights under the Copyright, Designs
and Patent Act 1988 to be identified as author of this work

Printed and bound by Baskerville Press, Salisbury, Wiltshire

All papers used by The Dovecote Press are natural, recyclable products
made from wood grown in sustainable, well-managed forests.

A CIP catalogue record for this book is available
from the British Library

1 3 5 7 9 8 6 4 2

CONTENTS

ACKNOWLEDGEMENTS

My thanks to John Goodwin for encouraging me to write in the first place and for all his help since. Thanks also to Roger Scott for his enthusiasm and encouragement. A big thank you to my wife Jill who has read everything I put in front of her and whose feedback and critical judgment have consistently proved correct.

Martin Munt, from Dinosaur Isle Museum, kindly read and corrected for technical accuracy the section on fossil-hunting. Tony Isaacs supplied up to date information on the cliffs from Freshwater to Alum Bay. Ventnor Heritage Museum have been helpful.

For illustrations I would like to thank Robin McInnes for permission to reproduce material from his books (pages 30, 41, 64, 72, 96, 103, 112, 114); Chris Ball for the engraving of Ryde Pier (page 13); Dinosaur Isle Museum for the ammonite and footprint (pages 28, 32); Richard Frost for the drawing of Mantell (page 29); Mr Morris of Brook for the photograph on page 83; Chuck Eccleston for his original photography (page 9); Roy Brinton for permission to reproduce the photographs on pages 43, 50, 71 and Hovertravel, Ryde, for the photograph on page 97.

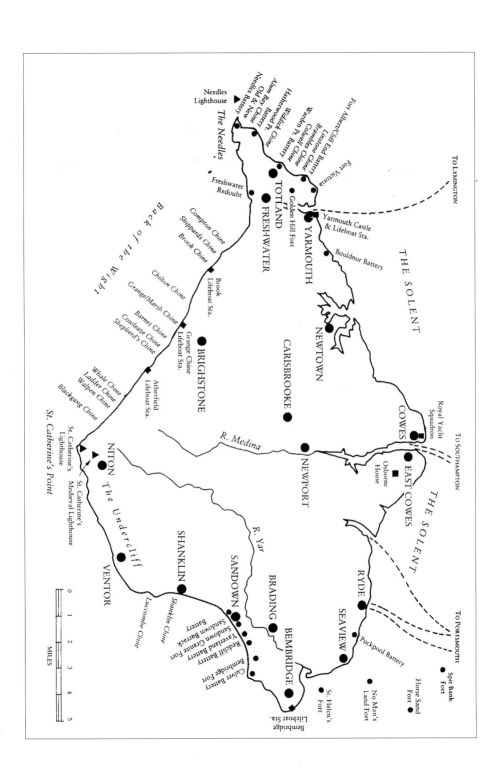

INTRODUCTION

WHERE sea and land meet is a very special place. An end and a beginning. The scene of partings and homecomings. Terra firma versus the relentless ocean. A conjunction of unique beauty, infinite variety and ever changing aspect that has provided inspiration for poets, writers and artists. For many who live and work by the sea a life away from the coast is unimaginable.

The sea takes and gives back. It bites chunks from the crumbling cliffs and builds beaches of breathtaking beauty. It has wrecked ships and taken lives, yielded a rich bounty and provided many with a livelihood. While erosion undermines the future, at the same time it delivers the key to the past by exposing the fossil record. The coast turned some folk into wreckers and opportunists for profit, others into unsung heroes battling the waves to save lives.

The seaside has furnished unforgettable holiday memories to generations of families and fulfilled the dreams of many in retirement. The coast is where fears of invasion brooded darkest and provided the stimulus to the building of defences. It is the interface of trade, legal and illicit. Yachts and boats are everywhere, symbol of man's amphibious tendencies.

The Isle of Wight, a rough diamond in shape and nature, has some 65 miles of coastline, 30 miles of which are designated 'Heritage Coast'. To the north the slippery fingers of harbours, creeks and tidal estuaries probe deep, threatening to slice the Island in half, but for man's intervention. To the south are sheer faces of white chalk, imposing bulwarks of red and yellow sandstone, shingle beaches stretching for miles beneath crumbling cliffs gashed by chines. 40 miles of this can be walked on public footpaths close to the coast and there is access to further isolated spots.

In this book I have looked at the Island's coast from many angles. Each chapter explores a different aspect with a lively mix of history, anecdote, fact and folk lore. I have not attempted to be comprehensive on each subject but rather have selectively dipped in to whet the appetite. At the end of the book there is a selection of suggested walks which encompass some of the material as well as linked attractions.

Shanklin Chine in the mid-nineteenth century.

COAST TO COAST

Island Connections

ABOUT 5,000 years ago the sea breached the wall of chalk that stretched from Dorset to the Needles, flooding the plain beyond and creating this island. Since that moment of separation boats of one kind or another have ferried goods and passengers across the Solent connecting us with them, island to mainland. Over the years the Solent 'passages' became well established. These routes and their points of departure and arrival remain largely the same today.

Nowadays the ferry companies are a favourite whipping boy, especially over fares that make the Solent mile for mile one of the most expensive stretches of water to cross in the world. This provides ammunition to advocates of a fixed link by way of a tunnel or bridge. So far the island has voted against such an irrevocable step. But proposals keep on surfacing.

The island lies close enough to the mainland for good communications and sufficiently distant to make the crossing special. For some visitors it is like going abroad; and for some islanders the mainland is 'England'. Porters embarking passengers on the ferry for Lymington would cry, 'This way to England!' and visitors to the island sometimes enquire whether they need a passport. A fixed link would change all that. The island would no longer be special, dividing us from them, islander from mainlander, 'caulkhead' from 'overner', and a whole tradition of the 'Solent passage' would be lost.

Sea Cabs and Horseboats

For many visitors their first glimpse of the Island's coastline is from the cosy lounge of a cross-Solent ferry. The comfort and ease of today's crossing is a far cry from the difficult and often hazardous affair of the past. In the days of Queen Elizabeth I passengers would often make a will before undertaking the voyage! Today we have hydrofoil and hovercraft, catamaran and car ferry. Before the advent of steam you could make the journey by one of the

A view of Ryde Pier and 'Horseboat Slip' with Victoria Pier on the right. Horseboats
were towed over from Portsmouth by steam tug and 'poled' onto the slipway.

sailing 'packets' that ran twice daily between Ryde and Portsmouth at a
single fare of 1/- in 1811, or by a Ryde wherry known as a 'sea cab'.

The wherry was a large two-masted open-decked sailing boat with oars for
windless days but offering little protection against the weather and sea spray.
Occasionally a tarpaulin across the deck would provide limited cover.
Accidents happened; in 1837 a wherry capsized in a squall on the Lymington
to Yarmouth passage drowning ten of the twelve passengers.

Ryde was the main landing point, and though embarkation was
straightforward at Portsmouth, at Ryde low tide exposed more than half a
mile of sand and mud for passengers and goods to negotiate. The novelist
Captain Marryat described how 'the wherries came in as far as they could
and were met by a horse and cart, which took out the passengers and carried
them through the mud and water to the hard ground'. Henry Fielding, the
author of *Tom Jones*, when bound for Lisbon in 1754 was lowered into a hoy
and rowed to shallow water to be hoisted by two sailors into a chair and
carried across the mud to shore. The opening of Ryde Pier in 1814 greatly

improved matters by permitting a more dignified landing at the cost of a 2d toll.

For many years cargo and livestock were carried in barges towed behind the sailing boats, although in bad weather passengers could find themselves sharing the boat with the stock. With the advent of steam specially constructed barges, known locally as 'horseboats,' were towed behind passenger steamers. This worked well enough until the arrival of the motor car.

Landing motor vehicles at Ryde in horseboats was a problem. The time of the service had to be changed daily so that the barge arrived on the top of the tide. The tug steamed for shore, cast off the tow boat and veered off at the last moment leaving the barge for the crew to pole on to the George Street slipway (now used by hovercraft). This primitive and somewhat hazardous routine ended in 1927 when Southern Railway built a deep water terminal at Fishbourne on Wootton Creek to take their new car ferry.

The Coming of Steam

Before the advent of steam even getting to the Isle of Wight was a lengthy affair. Travel to the ferry ports of Southampton and Portsmouth from London involved a laborious stagecoach journey of many hours with frequent stops to change horses and revive passengers. This was succeeded by a voyage of uncertain duration, the wherries being dependent on wind, tide and weather. Crossing times varied from one hour to Yarmouth from Lymington with a fair wind to the 'tedious passage of seven hours' endured by one luckless passenger in 1790 from Portsmouth to Cowes.

The first regular steam packet service across the Solent was started from Cowes in 1820. The *PS Arrow* and the *PS Union* started on the Ryde to Portsmouth route in 1825. There were four sailings daily and the fares were 1/6 (quarterdeck) and 1/- (forecastle). By 1830 the Yarmouth to Lymington run was being serviced by the steamship *Glasgow*.

Steam made a regular, reliable, timetabled service possible. The effect on Ryde as the main landing point for 'parties of pleasure' was dramatic. A local newspaper wrote in 1860 'all middle-aged inhabitants of Ryde can recollect the great excitement caused by the introduction of steam navigation to our waters . . . Ryde has been metamorphosed from a little fishing village with unpaved, unlighted and unwatched streets into a fashionable and aristocratic town.'

Ryde Pier with the Portsmouth steam packet alongside.

There was fierce competition between rival companies and much touting for business. Fights broke out between crews and touters of rival companies on the quayside. Collisions between steamers competing for berths were common and there was much public criticism of the state of some ships. Fare wars forced some companies to amalgamate or face liquidation. In 1861 two companies merged to form the Southampton, Isle of Wight & South of England Royal Mail Steam Packet Co. Ltd, now known as Red Funnel and still operating the Southampton to Cowes passage today. Steamer companies on the Ryde to Portsmouth passage were bought out by the joint railway companies (which became Southern Railway).

Southampton got its railway link in 1840, Portsmouth in 1847, though it was another 30 years before it was extended to the Harbour, and Lymington in 1858. The Rev E. Venables in his *Guide to the Isle of Wight* in 1860 wrote 'the establishment of the steam boat service . . . has rendered communication with the mainland regular and easy; while the various railroads . . . enable the traveller to reach the Isle of Wight from any part of England in the course of a few hours'.

This improvement in communications coincided with a sudden, rapid increase in the island's popularity. Physicians wrote about the island's healthy climate, attracting the wealthy to build villas and summer residences. Sea bathing and the seaside holiday were popularised by royalty, Cowes became the premier centre for yacht racing, and – above all – Queen Victoria built Osborne House, giving the Island fashionable respectability. The scene was set for the development of the Island's coastal resorts.

BESIDE THE SEA

The Development of the Holiday Resort

ONLY IN the last two hundred years has the coast become associated with health and recreation. Prior to that it was a place of seaports and fishing villages. The coast owes its rise in popularity to the vogue for sea bathing, which first attracted fashionable society, followed slavishly by the growing middle classes.

On the island Cowes and Ryde were the first to develop, being closest to the mainland and the easiest to get to. Cowes' prosperity was assured when the Royal Yacht Squadron moved there in 1826 and established the town as a centre for yacht racing. Ryde Pier was one of the first promenading piers and the town quickly became one of the most popular resorts in the country. Sir James Clark's championing of the health benefits of the Undercliff was the making of Ventnor. Sandown and Shanklin had to wait for the railways to arrive before their development began.

Health Spa to Holiday Resort

Up until the middle of the eighteenth century fashionable society took to the spa towns for health and recreation, to places like Bath and Cheltenham. The burgeoning middle classes followed the trends set by the fashionable oligarchy but spa water and spa towns were in limited supply. Seawater, however, was plentiful, and according to doctors salt water and bracing sea air were of inestimable benefit to health. Dr Russell's *A Dissertation on the Use of Sea Water in the Diseases of the Glands*, published in 1749, was an important influence in the development of seaside resorts.

Weymouth and Scarborough were flourishing resorts by 1780. Margate showed it's faith in the curative powers of sea water by founding in 1796 the Royal Sea Bathing Infirmary. Sea bathing was given royal approval when in 1789 George III bathed at Weymouth (while a band hidden in a neighbouring bathing machine struck up the National Anthem!).

It was a Margate man, the Quaker Benjamin Beale, who invented the bathing machine in the 1750s. The machines were wheeled down the beach and the occupants immersed in the sea by attendants for the good of their health. There were gentlemen's and ladies' machines, the latter sometimes with a modesty hood for privacy. In 1805 Ryde had one bathing machine; in 1811 there were eight. In 1860 there were three competing bathing establishments offering hot and shower baths as well as sea bathing. By the 1820s Cowes could offer bathing machines which were winched up and down the beach by a capstan. By the 1870s all the resort towns had bathing machines.

In 1829 Sir James Clark, later to become physician to the Queen, published *The Influence of Climate in the Prevention and Cure of Chronic Diseases.* A few years later he visited Ventnor and subsequently published a treatise, *On the Sanative Influence of Climate,* which included descriptions of the best resorts for invalids in England and southern Europe. Of Ventnor and the Undercliff he wrote, 'they bid fair to excel all other winter residences in this country, and the Isle of Wight will have added to its title of the 'Garden of England' that of the 'British Madeira'.

Further recommendation came from the Ventnor-based physician Dr George Martin in *The Undercliff of the Isle of Wight* (1849). In the wake of all this publicity Victorians rushed to build summer residences and lodging houses. Hotels went up to cater for the influx of visitors. Much of this building was speculative and unplanned and Ventnor grew higgledy piggledy up the hillside. With the coming of the railways in 1866 Ventnor's future was assured.

The benefits of sea bathing and a mild climate were not the only attractions of the growing seaside resorts; some had the added bonus of mineral springs like the traditional spa towns. Dr Fraser, physician to Charles II, discovered Shanklin's mineral springs, recommending its chalybeate waters for all cases of nervous exhaustion, anaemia, rheumatism and eczema. There were three main springs – at the head of the Chine, at Small Hope and below Osborne Steps. It was at Osborne Steps along Shanklin Esplanade that the Royal Spa Hotel was built in 1870, with the spring enclosed in a grotto to which only hotel visitors and subscribers had access.

At the turn of the twentieth century the Royal Spa Hotel had ladies and gentlemen's suites adjoining the hotel, each with two brass baths for iron water, hot and cold sea and freshwater baths, and large deep-water marble

The Royal Sandrock Hotel, Niton, in 1870.

baths. James Sampson at Fisherman's Cottage below the Chine was also offering hot or cold brine baths by the 1870s. Shanklin enjoyed the patronage of the Russian Imperial family and the German Princely Houses. The middle classes took their cue from the aristocracy and flocked to the seaside to breathe the ozone, plunge into baths, drink of the spa water, bathe in the sea or take health-giving genteel walks.

In 1807 a chalybeate spring was discovered between Niton and Blackgang by a Newport surgeon, Mr Waterworth. In a cottage above the spring he established a dispensary taking water direct from its source. A nearby private residence was converted into the Sandrock Hotel and a road built for access to the spring. In Dr. Martin's opinion the spring 'rivals the most famous in England' and the hotel proved popular. Following a visit by the Duchess of Kent and Queen Victoria it became the Royal Sandrock Hotel. It was destroyed by fire in 1984.

While visitors enjoyed the health benefits of the budding seaside towns they also wanted to be entertained and amused. Ever since the first visitors arrived the focal point had been the beach, where land and sea briefly overlap. The Victorians enjoyed the beach fully clothed, with hats and

Pierrots entertaining a crowd at
Seaview in the early 1900s.

parasols as a defence against the sun. Modesty required the use of a bathing machine or changing tent when going for a dip. These were supplied by fishermen, now 'longshoremen', who also provided deckchairs, canoes, rowing boats and sailing craft. In 1910 rowing boats could be hired at 1/- an hour (1/6 with a boatman) and a sailing boat at 2/6 an hour.

Troupes of pierrots and clowns, singers and travelling bands were licensed by the local council to perform on the shore and the esplanade. From 1864 Shanklin had a Town Band and two years later a Choral Society to provide regular entertainment. Pier pavilions, assembly rooms and theatres sprang up and by the early twentieth century were presenting concert parties, community singing, dancing and variety shows. There were of course the simple pleasures of promenading along pier or esplanade to watch and be watched, or digging in the sand, rockpooling, paddling and a curiously Victorian craze of pebbling. The health resort became the seaside resort and established itself at the centre of the British holiday tradition.

Paul Claudel in *A Frenchman in the Isle of Wight*, written following a visit in the late spring of 1889, paints a delicious picture of Victorian Shanklin.

'Life at an English seaside resort is one of adorable simplicity. Breakfast at nine, bathe at noon, luncheon at two, walk at four, flirt from morning to night, sleep from night to morning.

The view of the beach from our dining room window is one of feverish activity. A deep blue sea, all-of-a-sparkle with craft of every variety, bobbing heads, shouts, yells, windmill of arms, legs and oars. Now and then you catch a speck on the horizon – a man o'war from Portsmouth, or a liner from Southampton setting sail for southern seas.'

The Rise and Fall of Ventnor

At the beginning of the nineteenth century Ventnor was a hamlet of thatched fishermen's cottages with an old mill perched on a crag turned by a stream that fell in a cascade, a wayside inn and one or two humble dwellings. In the 1830s there was piecemeal growth and by 1838 the village had crept up to 350 souls. When Dr Lempriere talked of the 'striking advantage of the Undercliff climate' there was a trickle of visitors which became a flood when Sir James Clark eulogised Ventnor's healthy climate.

James Thorne, who wrote the Isle of Wight section in *The Land we Live in*, a 4-volume pictorial and literary history of the British Empire, says that 'Ventnor at once caught the attention of the crowd of visitors. In the tiny fishing hamlet soon sprang up hotels and boarding houses, shops and a church. Invalids came here for a winter retreat, as well as a summer visit. Speculation was stimulated. And now 'the plague of building' lighted on it, and it spread until every possible spot was planted with some staring building, or row of buildings. The variety of odd forms is remarkable. We have hotels, churches, shops, cottages, and villas in every conceivable style and every outrageous shape . . . Strawberry Hill Gothic, Seaside Swiss and Carpenters' palazzo.'

Ventnor in 1836, recalls Mark Norman, 'was spoken of far and wide as another 'El Dorado'.' In consequence there was a rush to it of 'all sorts and conditions of men. Amongst them were builders without capital or credit or character, speculators . . . who never raised a profit.'

By the 1840s it was clear that the growing town needed some organisation and a Ventnor Improvement Committee was formed. Roads were widened, new ones built, pavements laid and an Esplanade built. By 1851 the population had risen to 3,578 and some 76,000 people were conveyed by

Ventnor Esplanade was built between 1848 and 1850.

horse-drawn carriage between Ryde and Ventnor. Early moves to bring the railway to Ventnor were scotched by powerful men like John Hambrough, who had built Steephill Castle, and the Earl of Yarborough.

In 1864 the railway reached Shanklin. Two years later it was linked to Ventnor via a tunnel 1,312 yards long under the downs following well founded objections to the route via Luccombe. While the railway was under construction plans were put forward for a harbour formed by two breakwaters. It was completed well over budget and though steamers docked in it, bringing more visitors, the harbour was poorly built and quickly succumbed to the sea. To build the harbour a protective promontory known as Collins Point had been dynamited, so that once the two breakwaters had been destroyed Ventnor's beautiful shingle beach was swept away. At great cost protective groynes were built to help bring it all back.

William Spindler, the German millionaire who lived at Old Park, wrote a book in 1877 bemoaning the lack of foresight and initiative of Ventnor's residents. Compared with French watering places and English resorts like Bournemouth, Torquay and Brighton there was nothing for visitors to Ventnor to do! There were no Assembly Rooms suitable for concerts and public entertainments and no public pleasure gardens 'affording the invalid the essential boon of a quiet, sunny, and sheltered walk'.

Ventnor Pier and Esplanade Company began constructing a pier in 1871 but it wasn't fully completed, with a landing stage, until ten years later; it had been in use barely ten weeks when winter storms wrecked it. Amidst acrimony and dissent the Local Board bought the remains of the pier from the Company in order to continue the project, and finally the Royal Victoria Pier was opened in October 1887. Within two years 10,000 excursionists a year were visiting by steamer from Bournemouth, Southampton and Portsmouth. In 1906 the Pier Pavilion was built and the old pier bandstand removed to Ventnor Park. A second railway line from Newport to St Lawrence opened in 1897 and was extended to Ventnor West in 1900, bringing yet more visitors.

Ventnor's heyday was the Edwardian period from the turn of the century to the First World War. Visitors came by road, rail and sea to enjoy the beach and go bathing, promenade along the Esplanade or the pier and be entertained by German bands in Ventnor Park or by a concert party at the Pier Pavilion. Between the wars the Pavilion offered shows, tea dances, whist drives and community singing; in the winter the Pavilion was a rest room with games and periodicals and on Sundays a big crowd would listen to the Town Band. The need to constantly entertain visitors saw the Winter Gardens built in 1936.

After the war the pier was condemned but was rebuilt almost from scratch. The new pier, 683 feet long, was opened officially in May 1955. By September 200,000 had used it, including many thousands landed by steamer. The prosperity of the 1960s and cheap package holidays initiated the shift away from British resorts to sunnier climes abroad. The motor car finished off the railways, Ventnor West in 1952 and the main line from Ryde in 1966. The pier was demolished in 1993, leaving only a rump, but a new fair-weather harbour, Ventnor Haven, consisting of twin arms of granite blocks was completed in 2003 with hopes it would help regenerate the town.

Piers of the Realm

The Victorians liked their piers and no ambitious British seaside resort could afford to be without such a money-spinning attraction. Not only did they afford a delightful promenade out over the water; they provided the practical

Seaview Pier, modelled on Brighton's chain pier, in 1923.

function of a landing stage for the passenger ferries and excursion steamers that plied the coast depositing visitors with cash in their pockets.

Seaview Pier was built between 1879 and 1881 to allow visitors direct access from the mainland and tap in to the lucrative excursion trade. The elegant 1,000 feet long suspension pier had a gently undulating walkway along which pony-traps conveyed their passengers. It was modelled on the chain pier at Brighton and as a feat of engineering it was widely reported in the national press. In 1950 it was the first British seaside pier to be listed as a building of special architectural or historic interest but, within a month, it was washed away in the worst gales for 45 years.

The handsomest of the West Wight's piers is Yarmouth Pier, with it's smart lattice-work handrails. Recently restored, it consists of a walkway 609 feet long plus a T-shaped pier head. It was originally constructed by Yarmouth Corporation in 1875/6 as a deep water terminal for the cross-Solent steam packet service and as a berth for the increasing numbers of excursion steamers. It has the distinction of being the last remaining all wooden pier in Britain and a Listed Building. Restoration of the pier saw extensive use of a South American hardwood called greenheart that is so dense it will defy attempts by the gribble to eat it. The gribble is a saltwater version of the woodworm, with a stomach enzyme that can reduce wooden piles to pulp.

Shanklin Pier was famous for it's entertainment, especially in the 1920s and 30s when it was owned by Horace Terry Wood. The Casino Theatre in the new pavilion seated 1,000 people and held concert parties and Sunday attractions featuring stars of the day. In 1927 Anna Pavlova and the Corps de Ballet made an appearance and many household names of the period started their careers at Shanklin. Among the other amusements of the pier was a succession of performing divers – a one-legged diver called 'Professor Wesley' dived off a high platform in flames, another hurled himself off the pier on a bicycle. In the 1960s 'Dare Devil' Leslie would dive at any state of the tide, usually with the assistance of alcohol! Such entertainments came to an end at 2am on 16 October 1987 when a big storm destroyed the pier.

Ryde Pier was built in 1814 and was one of the first promenading piers in Britain. It is also one of the longest, only Southport and Southend stretch further out to sea. Originally 1,740 feet long it was extended to 2,250 feet in 1833 to allow steamers access at low tide. Furthermore it is not just one pier

Ryde Pier in 1864 showing the Horse Tramway.

but an agglomeration of structures. In 1864 a tramway pier was built alongside the existing one and in 1880 a railway pier was constructed next to that. A fourth pier, the Victoria, was completed in 1864 500 yards to the east but was a failure and was used as a bathing station. Tickets for the public baths at the pier head cost 6d in 1876 and were very popular. The Victoria Pier was demolished in 1916. The tramway, variously powered by horse, steam, electricity, petrol and diesel, was dismantled in 1969 leaving a gap between the promenade and railway pier.

Sandown Pier, with its elegant pair of toll booths and elaborate iron seats, opened in 1879 but the pier company failed and was taken over by a new company headed by Richard Webster, later created Lord Alverstone. In 1895 the new company lengthened the pier from 350 to 900 feet, built a grandiose pavilion and a landing stage for steamers. After the First World War the council bought the pier, enlarged the pavilion to seat 1,000 and presented highly successful summer shows. It was rebuilt in 1973 and sold to George Peak in 1986 who turned it into a sophisticated Space Age amusement park, a far cry from the slot machines and peep-shows of the past. This is the price of survival and Sandown Pier does survive against the odds, despite a fire in 1989 which required a £2 million refit.

'Any more for round the Island?'

Steam vessel excursions round the Island and to and from mainland resorts span over 150 years. The steamer excursion trade and pleasure piers grew in tandem. The growth in steamer traffic encouraged the building of piers which in turn allowed steamer companies to offer more trips with a greater variety of itineraries.

The paddle steamer *Medina* made the first steamer excursion around the Isle of Wight in September 1823 'crowded with fashionable persons of both sexes' and her example was quickly followed by others. These early circumnavigations were leisurely affairs taking from 6 to 7fi hours. In 1850 Round the Island excursions aboard the *Prince of Wales* or the *Princess Royal* cost 3/6 or 2/6 on the open deck. The popularity of sea excursions increased with the coming of the railways to Southampton and Portsmouth and the resultant rush of holidaymakers to the south coast.

Landing cruises or picnic excursions began in the 1830s, before the boom years of pier construction, and passengers were put ashore and re-embarked

Sandown sea front at the turn of the century had bathing machines,
rowing boats and sailing craft for hire.

by boat. The *Medina* was the first steamer to stop at Ventnor while on
excursion, anchoring in the bay in 1843 with 200 passengers and a band on
board. By the summer of 1854 the Ryde steamers were making a daily
excursion round the Island: 'A greater treat than which can scarcely be found
in the whole catalogue of steam boats in this country or on the Continent'.

Pleasure cruises reached their peak of popularity in the 1930s. During the
1934 season three companies had steamers call at Shanklin Pier, offering trips
to Brighton, Bournemouth, Southsea, Swanage, Round the Island, the
Needles, the Nab Tower, Portsmouth Harbour to see the battleships,
Southampton to see the liners and Cherbourg. The round trip to Cherbourg
was aboard the *Balmoral* and cost 12/6 with 2fi hours in France ashore.
Paddle steamers like the *Lorna Doone, Waverley, Balmoral, Southsea* and
Whippingham provided 'Round the Island' day trips, calling at other island
piers, and bringing mainland visitors for half day trips to the island.

Following the Second World War the paddle steamer excursion trade
struggled to survive. Piers that had been 'gapped' in the war were slow to be
rebuilt; Shanklin's pier wasn't restored until 1948. Government restrictions

The luxurious 427-ton paddle steamer *Lorna Doone* was a great favourite on Round the Island trips.

stifled the cross-Channel trade. Crew and fuel costs of steamers compared to motor vessels, combined with Board of Trade safety requirements, made the business less profitable. But the truth was that the expectations of the holidaymaker were also changing. The spartan comfort of the paddle steamer was no longer attractive and today's 'nostalgia' trade had yet to come into being.

WINDOW TO THE PAST

Fossil Hunting along the Coast

ONE HUNDRED and twenty million years ago the Isle of Wight was part of a large floodplain and swamp covering much of southern England. The climate was subtropical: hot and dry in summer, hot and wet in winter. There were meandering rivers, lakes and lagoons full of fish, turtles, crocodiles. In the wet season rivers became torrents of mud carrying plant and animal debris. On the coastlands were stands of conifers and giant ferns. Herds of plant-eating dinosaurs kept a wary look-out for their carnivorous cousins.

For millions of years dinosaurs ruled the earth. They lived and died and their bones were swallowed by swamp mud. Succeeding millennia buried this evidence under nearly a mile of later deposits. Then the enormous pressures which created the Alps and other mountain chains caused the folding and uplifting of rock strata here on the island. This combined with erosion by wind, rain and rivers exposed the dinosaur-bearing strata known as the Wessex Formation. Today there are outcrops of these rocks at Yaverland and a long stretch at the back of the Wight from Compton Chine to Atherfield Point.

The island is recognised as the best place in Europe for dinosaur remains. In terms of abundance, diversity and quality the rocks of the Isle of Wight yield dinosaur fossils of global importance. 26 species of dinosaur have been found on the island, several of them found nowhere else in the world – although some are known from only a few bones. The latest species to be discovered was *Eotyrannus*, an ancestor of *Tyrannosaurus*, in 2001. The Island's best kept secret is the location of the rare dinosaur *Neovenator* ('new hunter') as there are hopes of finding more remains in the cliffs.

Twice a day the sea plucks at the soft clay cliffs exposing fresh material. Some of this material succumbs to the sea and is washed away by the tide. Some finds its way into the hands of that curious breed, the amateur fossil hunter. The story of the dinosaurs is a detective story with *dramatis personae* as colourful and eccentric as Sherlock Holmes. How the dinosaurs came to light is as fascinating a tale as the story of the dinosaurs themselves. And the Isle of Wight played a key role.

'Hunting for old dragons'

Victorian clerics must have found their parishes less than taxing, for many had time for the scientific study of natural history. William Buckland was one such cleric, who later became Dean of Westminster Abbey. Although an eccentric who kept bears and jackals at his home, he was the first person to scientifically describe dinosaur remains, from a *Megalosaurus* found in Oxfordshire in 1824. Five years later he wrote a description of a large foot bone of an *Iguanodon* that had been found on the foreshore at Yaverland.

The *Iguanodon* is one of the best known dinosaurs and was among the first to be known from a complete skeleton and to be reconstructed in living form. It was one of three life size models of dinosaurs displayed at the Crystal Palace Exhibition in 1853/4, as a result of which it became world famous.

Fossil bones of *Iguanodon* are relatively common on the island. Indeed a

The footprint of an *Iguanodon*, a biped 30 feet long
and standing 18 feet high.

Gideon Mantell, doctor, geologist, museum curator,
writer and avid fossil-collector.

number of species were found here first and were thought to be unique to the island. *Iguanodon atherfieldensis* was named after a partial skeleton found at Atherfield Point in 1925 and discoveries continue to be made.

Iguanodon acquired its name through Gideon Mantell, physician, surgeon and amateur collector. One story has it that in 1822 Mantell's wife Mary Ann plucked a large fossil tooth from a pile of quarry stone used for road building while waiting for her husband who was attending a patient in Sussex. Tracing the rocks back to the quarry Mantell saw that large animals with these kind of teeth were unknown in rocks of that age.

Years later Mantell examined a preserved iguana from South America at the Museum of the Royal College of Surgeons. The teeth (for by now he had acquired more) appeared more like those of an iguana than any other animal so he named them *Iguanodon* or 'iguana's tooth', citing them as evidence of the existence of a giant prehistoric lizard.

Had he described the teeth when found Mantell would have beaten Buckland to the honour of first describing a dinosaur fossil. Mantell spent much time on the island and wrote several papers on Isle of Wight dinosaur fossils. But neither Buckland nor Mantell knew them then as dinosaurs for the word wasn't invented until 1841. That honour belongs to Richard Owen who used it in a lecture to the British Association for the Advancement of

Science when describing Buckland's and Mantell's finds. Because they defied classification Owen proposed a new class: Dinosauria, from the Greek for 'terrible lizard'. Owen was instrumental in establishing the Natural History Museum at South Kensington and is known to have visited and befriended the Rev William Fox, curate of Brighstone and one of the most prolific collectors of dinosaur bones.

The wife of the vicar of Brighstone said of Fox 'it's bones first the parish next'. Fox's impact on the study and discovery of dinosaurs is unparalleled. He discovered more species than anyone else in the UK and has more dinosaurs named after him than any other Englishman. Fox would ride out to the cliffs on his donkey to search for bones at favourite places like Barnes High. His impressive collection of over 500 specimens was acquired by the Natural History Museum on his death.

His most famous discovery was *Polacanthus foxi*, a plant-eating armoured dinosaur with a double row of sharp pointed spikes down its back. His other finds include *Aristosuchus* ('superior crocodile') and *Hypsilophodon foxi*

A fossil collector removing a specimen from fallen boulders at Ventnor.

('high crowned tooth'), both only found on the Isle of Wight.

Fox kept company with some of the great Victorian scientists and was a friend of Alfred Lord Tennyson. When his position as curate was under threat Owen interceded for him and even wrote to Gladstone on his behalf. Fox wrote to Owen, 'I cannot leave this place while I have any money left to live on, I take such deep pleasure in hunting for old dragons.'

Recently films and TV have popularised dinosaurs to an unprecedented extent and today the island has two excellent centres. Dinosaur Isle Museum at Sandown incorporates the old Museum of Isle of Wight Geology to provide a modern visitor centre dedicated to Isle of Wight dinosaurs and featuring life-sized models. The Dinosaur Farm Museum at Brighstone boasts a display of part of a *Brachiosaur*, the largest dinosaur found on the Island. At both centres visitors can see and talk to experts at work on the latest finds.

'Shepherds' Crowns' and 'Sand Dollars'

Dinosaur remains are not the only fossils to be found on the Isle of Wight. Other creatures from different periods have also found their way into the fossil record. Most are found in sedimentary rocks, the result of deposition, such as on the sea bed (and are therefore of marine animals). Some clays, sands and gravels laid down in lakes and rivers contain freshwater life and the bones of animals that died or fell in. The Isle of Wight has almost a complete sequence of sedimentary rocks from 120 million years ago to now.

So what exactly are fossils? They are the remains of animals and plants preserved in rocks – usually the hard bits like bone, shells, teeth etc. Moulds and casts sometimes preserve the shape of a creature when all other remains have disappeared. Trace fossils are fossils of an animal's activity not the creature itself, such as tracks or footprints. Rocks of the same age contain the same fossils. It is therefore possible to date a bed of rock by its fossils and likewise to anticipate the fossil record from knowledge of the rocks.

The most spectacular example of plant fossils is visible at low tide off the rocks at Hanover Point, Brook. Known as the Fossil Forest or Pine Raft, it consists of petrified giant conifers and, more rarely, pineapple-shaped cycads. They were first discovered by Thomas Webster, a naturalist, in 1813 but it was Gideon Mantell who understood how they came to be there. 'The trees evidently originated in a raft composed of a prostrate pine forest, transported from a distance by the river which flowed through the country . . . and became submerged in the sand and mud of the delta'. Petrified pine cones can also be found on the beach and hazel nuts, known locally as 'Noah's nuts' from the gravels in the clifftop.

If one single image epitomises the world of fossils it is the coiled segmented shell of the ammonite. They appear in walls and gardens, on display on shelves and windowsills. The ammonite takes it's name from the Egyptian God Amon who was often depicted wearing a headdress of coiled ram's horns. They were phenomenally successful creatures, and are related to the nautilus found swimming in the Pacific today. Like the dinosaurs, they disappeared inexplicably from the fossil record 65 million years ago.

Ammonites have been known up to two metres across, but the largest found on the island is about the size of a car tyre! The area around Whale Chine in Chale Bay is the place to look and there are two main shape varieties – tightly coiled, round ammonites and open coiled ammonites shaped like a sea horse. An unusual ammonite that coils upwards like a snail can be found at Culver Cliff and St Catherine's Point.

Ammonites as big as one metre across have been found at Blackgang.

Crustaceans such as lobsters, prawns and crabs aren't common as fossils because they tend to break up. However amongst the greyish clay cliffs of Atherfield 110-million-year-old lobsters have been found perfectly preserved in every detail. Equally rare are fossils of fish, but just down the road at Compton and Brook Bay you may come across the scales or teeth of an armoured fish that was a contemporary of dinosaurs. The fish, *Lepidotes mantelli*, owes its name to Gideon Mantell and the round, black, shiny teeth are known to locals as 'fish eyes'.

More colourful names have been acquired by commonly found fossils such as sea urchins. Round ones are popularly known as 'shepherds' crowns', heart-shaped as 'fairy hearts' and flattened ones as 'sand dollars'. Perhaps the most curious finds of all are off Hamstead beach. Crocodile droppings have been found here, croissant-shaped and containing fish remains! You may also find crocodile's teeth and their bony scales known as scutes.

Believe it or not crocodile droppings are one of the many fossils you can buy at Martin Simpson's Fossil Shop at Blackgang. Such is Martin's reputation that the Post Office frequently forward letters to him addressed simply as 'The Fossil Man, Isle of Wight'. He brings a light hearted approach to his subject and his fossil hunting expeditions are popular with schools.

Martin is author of a highly readable and indispensable practical guide called *Fossil Hunting on Dinosaur Island*, and testimony to his enthusiasm for them lies in the 36,000 specimens weighing nearly 40 tonnes that he keeps at home!

BEACONS AND BARRACKS

Invasion threats & Coastal defences

THE ISLAND is no stranger to influx and invasion, peaceful or bloody. Some invaders reached our coast intent on conquest and settlement; others landed to raid and pillage, or to terrorise in the name of king or country. Sometimes the island was the objective; at other times it was used as a stepping stone to threaten the bigger prize across the Solent. In medieval times fear of invasion was so widespread that measures had to be taken to prevent the depopulation of the Isle of Wight. False alarms sent jitters down the island's spine. In their time, Roman galley, Viking long boat, French raider and Spanish galleon have all threatened the island's coast.

'Danger of a hostile descent'

The island was first settled by Celts from northern France, followed by the Belgae. In AD 43 the Romans invaded Britain and the island, which the Romans called Vectis, fell peacefully to Vespasian. The Romans ruled for 400 years bringing stability, order, peace and prosperity. There is certainly no evidence that the inhabitants found Roman rule oppressive. As the power of the Roman empire declined, it was threatened by invaders, ultimately surrendering far-flung outposts like Britain. In AD 410 the Romans withdrew and the 'Dark Ages' began.

Gradually the Romans were replaced by the Jutes, Angles and Saxons. In AD 530 the West Saxon leaders Cerdic and Cynric invaded, bringing the island under the rule of Wessex. The *Anglo Saxon Chronicle* states that many were killed at Carisbrooke and just 4 years later a fresh slaughter took place when the island was given to Stuf and Wihtgar, Cerdic's nephews. It is from Wihtgar that the name Wight is derived.

In due course the Vikings began mounting raids on Britain. In 897 during King Alfred's dogged resistance to the Danes, six Viking ships put ashore at Brading and fighting followed. Three escaped but went aground and the survivors of the ensuing skirmish were hanged at Winchester. A hundred years later the Vikings were using the island as a base for raids along the south coast, wintering at Werrar, a muddy creek on the west bank of the Medina River.

Security from the Viking marauders came with the Norman Conquest, which brought order and stability until the fourteenth century. As the Normans' links with France weakened so fear of French invasion grew. In 1324 a total of 31 warning beacons was established across the island, the first in England. In an attempt to stiffen the island's defences Edward III declared that no one could leave it on pain of forfeiting their property.

From 1337 England was at war with France on and off for over a hundred years and French raids were expected at any time. In 1340, after a number of minor incursions, the French landed at St Helens. Sir Theobald Russell as 'Captain of the Men of the Wight' was killed leading a successful counter-attack.

In the same year the old town of Wolverton near Brading was laid waste. The town had access to the sea, ramparts for defence on the landward side and a chapel for worship called St Urian's (from which Centurion's Copse, the site of Wolverton, is corrupted). One version of events relates how a hermit, living in a cave on Culver Cliff, spotted the French ships approaching round Dunnose and head for the beach at Sandown. He ran to the town to raise the alarm but nobody believed him. The town was attacked from Sandown and by forces that had rowed up from St Helens, overwhelmed and burnt to the ground. It was never rebuilt.

In the reign of Edward III effective defence was organised. Lords of the manor and clergy raised men-at-arms and archers who were reinforced by a hundred slingers and archers from London. Edward III's military success in France caused simmering resentment and throughout the 1370s the island daily expected invasion.

Following a number of minor landings the threatened attack came. In August 1377 a combined French and Spanish fleet landed at Yarmouth and razed it along with Francheville (Newtown) and Newport. The inhabitants fled to Carisbrooke Castle where Sir Hugh Tyrrel organised the defence.

The French stayed a month beseiging the castle. Some were ambushed and slaughtered in a narrow lane thereafter called Deadman's Lane (now Trafalgar Road) in honour of another more decisive victory over the French and Spanish. The French were further disheartened when their leader was killed by Peter de Heyno, a militia leader and lord of the manor of Stenbury, who shot him with his silver crossbow through a loophole in the west side of the castle, which is known to this day as 'Heynoe's Loope'. The French decided to withdraw when the beleagured islanders paid them off with a thousand marks.

It was said that no-one set foot in Newport for two years while Newtown and Yarmouth languished. A petition to Parliament in 1378 tells of 'the greater part of the inhabitants' having 'left the island from the great damages received from the enemy's fleet'. Land was left uncultivated and industry suffered. In 1402 the French were back with 1,700 men and burnt two villages. In 1403 the French leader St Pol and 1,000 men landed intent on stealing cattle but were forced back to their ships by the militia. They returned the following year probing the defences but taking care to avoid clashing with the militia.

Until English naval supremacy was established the island remained a frontier zone and the need for a strong militia was a constant preoccupation. Measures were taken to encourage settlers on the island. On the accession of Queen Elizabeth I the island's condition was such that a commission was appointed to investigate the cause and found demoralisation and neglect due to 'the constant state of alarm in which the inhabitants lived from the danger of a hostile descent'.

The last and greatest raid on the island came in 1545 when Francis I of France launched an invasion in reply to Henry VIII's own incursions at Calais a year earlier. A fleet of 150 battleships, 60 pinnaces and 25 galleys under Admiral Claude d'Annebault arrived off the island in July. This must have been an impressive and frightening sight. They headed for Portsmouth where Henry VIII was reviewing a fleet which included the warship the *Mary Rose*. During a minor skirmish the king was a spellbound witness to the tragic sinking of the *Mary Rose*. Heeled over in the wind, unsecured cannon crashed across the decks forcing her lower gun ports below water.

The French turned their attention to the island, landing 2,000 men at three different spots – Seaview, Bembridge and Bonchurch. At Seaview they took the fort and followed the defenders as they fled into Priory Woods, killing many and then burning Nettlestone. The largest force landed at Bembridge and a skirmish took place on the slopes of Bembridge Down before the French retired to their ships having burnt Bembridge and Yaverland. The third force landed at Bonchurch where they were met by men of the

Hampshire militia and another skirmish ensued.

In 1582 Sir George Carey became Captain of the Isle of Wight and with invasion still threatening he set about restoring the medieval beacon system, so that information on the strength of an enemy fleet could be relayed across the island and on to the mainland. Discipline was strict, the watchmen were subject to regular inspections and were required to blow whistles every fifteen minutes to prove they were awake!

Sir George also set about improving defences, providing more muskets for his men and better training. Almost a fifth of the island's population were in training with the militia. The threat of invasion was taken seriously. From 1587 a Spanish invasion was expected and the Isle of Wight was considered a main objective.

The attack came next year in 1588 when Philip of Spain sent an armada of 130 ships up the Channel. Philip had discussed capture of the island as a secondary objective and it formed part of the overall plan. 'If the principal design should fall through, it would be very influential in bringing them to the best conditions possible, if the armada were to take possession of the Isle of Wight. If this once be captured, it could be held, and would afford a shelter to the armada, whilst the possession of it would enable us to hold our own against the enemy.'

On the 25 July, with beacons flaring along the south coast, the Spanish fleet was sighted off the island. An engagement took place off Dunnose in a calm sea of which Sir George Carey wrote, 'this morning began a great fight betwixt both fleets south of this island . . . with so great expense of powder and bullet that during the said time the shot continued so thick together that it might have been judged a skirmish with small shot on land than a fight with great shot at sea'. Militia and inhabitants no doubt watched with bated breath. The Armada was harried on up the Channel and round Scotland to an ignominious end.

The island remained nervous of invasion long after the Armada. Sir John Oglander recalls that in 1624 thirty merchant ships from Hamburg lay off St Helens when rumours spread that the Hamburghers were invading. Panic set in and the beacon was fired. The alarm was raised in Portsmouth, King James informed in London and the fleet readied. Sir John records that 'old William Scott, aged 89, having been some 5 years bedridden, upon the alarum got out of bed and walked 3 miles. Fear maketh a man to forget both age and sickness'. When all calmed down the man who lit the beacon found himself

Charles Dumouriez, the French soldier who
in 1777/8 prepared a plan for the invasion of
the Isle of Wight by the French.

in Carisbrooke Castle prison! Four years later a similar alarm raised the whole south coast of England.

In the eighteenth century it was the French again who troubled English minds, not without reason. During the war with the American colonies the French politician and soldier of fortune Charles Dumouriez prepared an elaborate plan for the invasion of the Isle of Wight. The plan hinged on commandeering two hundred of the Cherbourg peninsular's oyster ketches as troop transports. The main force was to land at Sandown, whose fort was garrisoned by only 150 troops. Once the island was taken it was to be turned into a fortress. The plans however were left to gather dust. Bonaparte revived the idea to invade Britain using flotillas of barges to carry his troops across the Channel but Nelson scuppered his plans at Trafalgar.

In July 1940 Hitler issued a directive ordering an invasion of England. 'The landing will be in the form of a surprise crossing on a wide front from about Ramsgate to the area west of the Isle of Wight . . . The possible advantages of limited operations before the general crossing (eg. the occupation of the Isle of Wight . . .) are to be considered from the point of view of each branch of the armed forces and the results reported to me'.

The possibility of invasion was taken so seriously that an underground resistance unit was trained in sabotage techniques intended to tie down any occupying forces. Anti-invasion obstacles were built on beaches, including scaffolding barriers the whole length of Sandown Bay. Cement blocks known as 'dragon's teeth' were placed on the beaches as defence against tank landings and sections were removed from the middle of piers to prevent their use. Pill boxes were constructed, coastal batteries reactivated and the sea forts equipped with searchlights to help the shore batteries find their targets.

Invasion by sea may not have materialised but invasion by air was a reality. In one terrible air raid on Cowes on the night of 4/5 May 1942 68 civilians were killed, many injured and parts of the town destroyed. The air raid sirens sounded a total of 1,594 times during the war, including on 55 consecutive days and nights between 18 March and 11 May 1941.

Sandown's three forts

With its wide sandy beach Sandown has always been considered a good landing place for invading forces. As protection against French raids Henry VIII ordered a fort to be built there, though it was too late to be of use against the French landing of 1545. This first fort, quadrangular with four towers, was provided with '11 pieces of brass and iron ordnance, 605 shot of various sorts and sizes, with 12 hollow shots for powder, 78 hagbutts, a chest of bows and another of arrows, 150 pikes, and 120 bills'. It was manned by a captain, lieutenant, 13 soldiers, a porter, master gunner and 7 gunners. But in less than a hundred years it was swallowed by the encroaching sea, and its foundations can be seen today only with the aid of mask and snorkel at low water spring tides opposite the old coastguard cottages.

In 1632, during the reign of Charles I, the old fort was dismantled before it disappeared beneath the waves and a second fort was built known as the Star Fort. Sir John Oglander and Sir John Dennis as overseers wrangled with the appointed engineers arguing that their siting of the fort just 80 yards from the beach was too close to the sea and it would suffer the same fate as its predecessor. It was lucky to survive a different threat when the Master Gunner in charge went mad, killed his wife and children and threatened to blow himself up in the magazine. During the War with the American colonies the fort was attacked by ambitious privateers without success.

There is a magnificent engraving by Richard Livesay entitled *Grand Review at Sandham Bay* in which the second fort is depicted (see p. 41). The

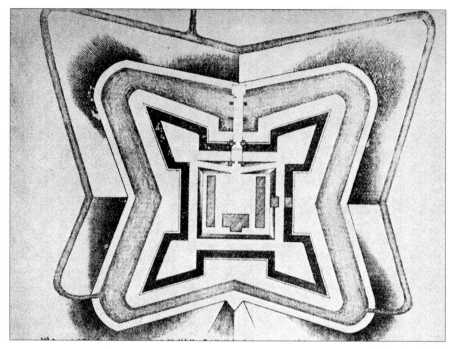

Plan of Sandown 'Star' Fort, built in 1632.

engraving shows General Sir William Pitt, Commander in Chief of the South Western District, reviewing the troops at Sandown Fort in 1798. Ranks of soldiers stretch in an almost uninterrupted arc along the golden sands and up onto Bembridge Down. On the beach is an artillery piece, the crew standing to attention. The tents of a substantial encampment can be seen in the distance. The review party dressed in colourful uniforms hold their horses in check while discussing manouevres.

The review was part of the island's preparations to meet the threat of invasion by Napoleon's Grand Army. The scale of the manoeuvres shows that the threat was taken seriously. Brick barracks were built along the coast for 300 men at Sandown, 150 at Colwell, 50 at Compton and Grange Chines and 50 at Niton. There were 4,500 troops from the mainland stationed on the island and with 3,000 inhabitants under arms the Isle of Wight was one huge garrison.

In Queen Victoria's reign invasion scares prompted Lord Palmerston to set up a Royal Commission to review the country's defences. The outcome was the construction in 1866 of a third fort built of granite, with twelve guns

Richard Livesey's engraving, *Grand Review at Sandham Bay*, shows General Sir William
Pitt reviewing troops at Sandown Bay during the Napoleonic Wars
when the threat of invasion was real.

behind armour shields in 'casemates' whose role was to oppose ships in the
bay while three shore batteries were to cover beach landings. The second fort
was dismantled, but when the granite fort fell out of use it proved impossible
to demolish and has found a new life as home to the Isle of Wight Zoo.

The Needles Passage

Once Portsmouth became established as Britain's main naval base the
approaches to it had to be defended. With a south west wind and strong
currents in their favour an invader could rapidly make it past the Needles and
the narrows at Hurst to threaten Portsmouth via 'the back door'. The
development of cannon gave opportunities to shore-based batteries for
defence; so to defend the Needles Passage, fortifications were built west of
Yarmouth. The shipping channel narrows here to less than a mile wide,
squeezed between Hurst Spit and the island, bringing shipping within

artillery range.

The first defensive work in the area was erected midway between Sconce Point and Cliff End. James Worsley, when Captain of the Isle of Wight, constructed a small stone tower in 1525. It was octagonal in shape with cannon mounted on the roof and described by the Earl of Southampton as 'one of the worst devised things I have seen'. It soon fell out of use and nothing remains today but a name on the map, Round Tower Point, between Forts Victoria and Albert.

In 1547 James Worsley's son Richard, as Captain of the Wight, nicknamed 'The Fortifier', built Yarmouth Castle and Sharpnode Blockhouse at Sconce Point opposite Henry VIII's new castle on Hurst Spit. In a survey of 1559 the only member of the Sharpnode garrison was Walter Basse, master gunner, who earned 6d a day. Under Sir George Carey, Sharpnode was replaced by a new fort that was the work of another Worsley (Thomas) and John Dingley. This was a five pointed star fort and dubbed Carey's Sconce (after the Dutch word 'schans' meaning fort).

Another survey of 1623 described the fort as 'nothing but a bare model of an old ruynated Sconce which hath been many yeares utterly abandoned'. It remained in disuse until fear of invasion during the Napoleonic Wars goaded the island to replace Carey's Sconce with an open-topped redoubt covering nearly half an acre and known as Sconce Point Battery. With the defeat of Napoleon in 1815 the battery became a coastguard station.

In 1851 Louis Napoleon, nephew of the great Napoleon, came to power in a 'coup d'etat'. Once again fear of invasion mounted. In response, coastal defences were bolstered and work began on Fort Victoria on top of Sconce Point Battery, having first evicted Joseph Russell, a senior coastguard boatman, who had been living there with his wife and 7 children. Two years later work started on Fort Albert at Cliff End, south of Round Tower Point. Simultaneously, Freshwater Redoubt was constructed on the western headland of Freshwater Bay to prevent troops landing on the beach and marching on both forts from the rear.

These defences were heavily criticised by the Scottish architectural writer James Fergusson who visited Fort Victoria while work was in progress. Fergusson was a supporter of earthwork defences rather than masonry coastal forts and he later wrote a severely critical pamphlet which attracted some bitter correspondence in the *Times*. Fergusson was to be proved right. Advances in technology saw the introduction of rifled breech-loading guns

Golden Hill Fort, built between 1863-7, was the headquarters of the Western District School of Gunnery from 1888 till the outbreak of the Second World War.

firing elongated explosive shells that could rip the masonry walls apart. Both Fort Victoria and Fort Albert were white elephants within a decade.

The launching by the French of the first steam ironclad warship in 1859, together with advances in artillery, sparked another invasion scare and led Lord Palmerston to set up a Royal Commission on the Defences of the United Kingdom: among it's members was James Fergusson. In the Report Forts Victoria and Albert were described as 'not of the most approved construction' and in 1876 the Defence Committee recommended Fort Victoria's demolition. Instead, both forts were downgraded for use primarily as barracks and storehouses and taken out of front line service.

Following the Report four new clifftop batteries were built at Needles Point, Hatherwood Point, Warden Point and Cliff End to deter an enemy from attempting the Needles Passage. To protect these batteries from attack from the rear a barracks and fort were built at Golden Hill. The 1890s saw the development of quick-firing guns that could fire up to 25 shells a minute. The old batteries were altered to take these guns and a new battery was constructed at New Needles. One further battery was added to this coastline in 1937 at Bouldnor.

Some of these fortifications have been preserved and are open to the public. The Needles Old Battery is in the hands of the National Trust who have rescued two of the original gun barrels from the sea and remounted them. Yarmouth Castle is well preserved and the tiny Great Hall, master gunner's parlour and gun platforms are on show. Fort Victoria is now a Country Park and Fort Albert a block of luxury apartments. Fort Redoubt was opened as a tea room but has reverted to a private residence. A stone plinth that was used by the gunners at Freshwater to set their landward limit during practise firings can still be seen at Hanover Point, Brook.

Palmerston's Follies

The Royal Commission set up by Lord Palmerston to look into Britain's defences made sweeping recommendations. To protect the Spithead entrance and defend Portsmouth Naval Dockyard from bombardment three granite sea forts were erected, in the 1860s, on shoals – Spit Bank, No Man's Land and Horse Sand. A fourth was built later off St Helens to protect the anchorage. The sea forts were supported by a battery of mortars at Puckpool.

To prevent an enemy landing at Sandown and taking Puckpool from the rear the town's defences were strengthened. Three new batteries were constructed at Redcliff, Yaverland and Sandown Barracks to deliver a crossfire onto the beaches while the Granite Fort, which replaced the Star

A gun barrel being moved by troops during alterations to
Puckpool Battery around 1898.

Fort, opposed enemy ships with its guns.

To support these defences a hexagonal land fort with brick-lined ditches was built on Bembridge Down at a cost of £49,000. The siting of the fort meant moving an obelisk commemorating the Earl of Yarborough, the first Commodore of the Royal Yacht Squadron. The Commission had proposed building a series of towers along the south coast but these plans were dropped. A Military Road was constructed to hasten the movement of troops from one end of the island to the other.

Anti-invasion barriers in Sandown Bay during the
Second World War. Notice the gap in the pier; all piers
were 'sectioned' as a precaution against landings.

Palmerston was criticised for building unnecessary defences against a largely illusory enemy at enormous cost. One critic, Bernal Osborne, quoted Gibbons:

'To raise this fortress of enormous Price,
The head of Folly used the hand of Vice'

Osborne declared that though no vice was in question, it was certainly folly to spend millions on such forts. And so they were branded Palmerston's Follies.

Bembridge Fort was bought by the National Trust in 1965 and is now unused. All the sea forts were put up for sale and are now in private hands or under the management of Portsmouth Dockyard Property Trust. Puckpool battery is now a park run by the Council. All that remains of some batteries are the concrete gun emplacements; in the case of Redcliff and Hatherwood even that has succumbed to cliff erosion.

CHINES, CLIFFS, CREEKS AND CAVES

The shape of the coast and life at the sea's edge

THE SEA is both destroyer and builder. What the sea erodes it deposits elsewhere. Waves eat away the land at different rates depending on the hardness of the rock; resistant rocks like chalk stand out as headlands while softer material is scooped out as bays and coves. Over the years rock is ground to a fine consistency and settles on the sea bed, but coarser material from sand to pebbles moves to and fro along the shore. Bays like Sandown Bay between headlands will accumulate a crescent of sand or shingle, whilst spits form across the mouths of estuaries. Along the 'Back of the Wight' the cliffs are scored by deep gorges known as chines.

Of all the island's coastline the most imposing and grand are the chalk cliffs at the eastern and westernmost points of the island. Spectacular walls of perpendicular white chalk have been sculpted by the sea and weathered into bluffs and arches, ledges and caverns, pinnacles and stacks. Many of these features have names and a tale to tell.

In contrast to the high cliffs and coves of the south coast the north coast slopes gently to the Solent. Where the north flowing rivers meet the shore a number of broad estuaries have formed. The low crumbling cliffs are composed of sands and clays and are eroded by the sea, which then flows into the estuaries laden with silt. This settles to form mudbanks. In the calm waters of the estuary, protected by spits, the mudbanks build. Estuaries like Newtown have a range of nationally important habitats – tidal mudflats, saltmarsh, lagoons, shingle banks and spits.

Chines

Chines are narrow ravines or gorges formed by the rapid erosion of soft clays and sands caused by water flowing out towards the sea. 'Chine' is an old English word derived from the Anglo Saxon *cinan*, meaning to chink, split or rive. It is peculiar to Hampshire, Dorset and the Isle of Wight. There are 19 chines on the island stretching from Shanklin to just west of Yarmouth.

Chines provided shelter and water to early human communities and provide the same to wildlife today. Each has it's own character and own habitat. For centuries they have provided the means of access to the beach through the crumbling cliffs. Smugglers used them to land their contraband. Lifeboats have been launched from them. The local inhabitants used them to spirit away the harvest of the sea from wrecks. Geologists have found in them a window to the past. Today they are enjoyed for their natural beauty.

The chine has long been Shanklin's most famous natural feature. From the late eighteenth century travellers in increasing numbers came to admire it's natural beauty. It's a particularly deep chine sheltered from the prevailing wind, enabling woodland to grow. A stream cascades down the steep ravine and in the cool moist environment ferns and mosses thrive.

Shanklin Chine in 1847.

Luccombe Chine and the fishing community on the shore in 1839.

In 1817 William Colenutt built Fisherman's Cottage at the mouth of the chine. Four years later, he cut a path up through it and gained the permission of Mrs Walton White, the lady of the manor, to act as a guide to visitors and charge for the service. By 1860 its wildness had been tamed. Venable's *Guide to the Isle of Wight* notes locked gates at the entrances where a janitor 'waits to admit you on the receipt of a slender fee. Happily the locked gate is the extent of the evil'. A representative of *Punch* magazine whined in 1873 that 'I had to pay eighteen pence for seeing this Shanklin toy'. Now it is floodlit at night, turning its wild beauty into a funfair attraction.

Smuggling was rife in Shanklin and the chine was one of several routes for transporting tubs of spirits off the beach. The Chine Inn was a noted haunt of fishermen and smugglers. So serious was the problem that excisemen were stationed at Jessamine Cottage in the old village and from 1820 at the Watch House on the shore. The wide cliff walks such as Keats Green above the chine were the result of field boundaries set back from the cliff edge to allow patrolling mounted Revenue Officers an unimpeded ride!

The chine played a role in the Second World War. It was used as an assault course by Commandos in training for the Dieppe raid of 1942. It was at Shanklin Chine that PLUTO (Pipeline under the Ocean) left island shores for France, pumping petrol across the Channel to fuel the Normandy landings at the rate of 56,000 gallons a day.

Luccombe Chine is a handsome cleft with a rivulet tumbling onto the beach and flanked by towering sandstone cliffs that enclose a secluded bay. In the mid-nineteenth century there was an undercliff or terrace on which was perched a group of fishermens' cottages and even a small chapel. Five families were known to live at Luccombe – the Kingswells, Kemps, Buttons, Casses and Tom Hardy. They scratched a living from casual labour on nearby estates, fishing and potting, and no doubt a little smuggling. The buildings succumbed to a landslide in February 1910.

Venables in his *Guide* of 1860 calls Blackgang Chine 'one of the great lions . . . which everybody sees, and with which almost everybody is disappointed'. You enter by a 'kind of toy-shop or bazaar from which visitors are expected to make some trifling purchase' to gain access to the paths. How much more disappointing today with a sprawling theme park instead of savage beauty.

In the wake of the success of Shanklin Chine Alexander Dabell, son of a Nottingham lacemaker, bought Blackgang and opened it to the public in 1843.

Alexander Dabell bought the chine and opened it to the public in 1843. It remains in family hands, a changing mix of funfair, light entertainment and learning experience.

From the beach you can see how Blackgang gained its name. Wet sooty black cliffs retain a raw and awesome grandeur. A way, or 'gang' once wound up through the chasm but the cliff has retreated leaving a sheer drop and the path is gone. It was here that the *Clarendon* was wrecked in 1836 with the loss of 23 lives, prompting the building of St Catherine's Lighthouse.

Walpen Chine takes its name from nearby Walpen Farm, which was mentioned in the Domesday Book. It's neighbour, Ladder Chine, is so called from the only mode of descent in former years, but in the 1930s there was a good path down to the beach. Today there is no way down through either chine, which are now no more than bowl-shaped depressions sculpted out of the cliff face.

James Wheeler's log records in 1758 a beached whale 63 feet long 'between Old Node and Mackerel Rails', and many believe it to be the origin of the name Whale Chine. However it is more likely to refer to the local Wavell (pronounced wa-ull) family who owned nearby Atherfield Farm between 1557 and 1636. Whale Chine is the most impressive chine at the 'back of the Wight', a large gash in the cliff with sheer sides and nearly 200 feet wide at the mouth.

Heading west round Atherfield Point you encounter Shepherd's Chine and Cowleaze Chine, two broad, shallow chines with grassy sides. They were formed by a stream rising near Kingston which now runs through Shepherd's but once ran through Cowleaze. The former supposedly owes its name to a shepherd who wanted to net the eels found in the mud of the stream in the 1790s and diverted it's course with the intention of restoring it. Heavy rains deepened the channel making restoration impossible and the new chine was named after its unintentional creator.

Barnes Chine is little more than a cleft in the cliff today but when Hassell undertook his tour of the island in 1790 'Barns Hole' was a 'vast chasm . . . The entrance has the appearance of leading to some subterraneous passage which furnishes a retreat for a nest of robbers'. Even further back in time around 1200 BC a Bronze Age community had their cemetery here, a circle of graves, but all trace has been washed away by the sea. Off the chine lies a reef marked on old charts as Ship Ledge, but which since the loss of a Dutch vessel here has become known locally as Dutchman's Hole.

Below Brighstone is the broad trough of Grange Chine, with it's smaller cousin Marsh Chine filtering into it. Grange refers to a monastic farm near here in medieval times. Both Hassell and Venables in their tour guides refer to it as Jackman's Chine. Could this be the same man Bromfield mentions in his *Flora Vectensis*? – 'Jackman, an intelligent cliffsman, whom I have repeatedly employed to procure specimens (of sea stock) from their otherwise inaccessible location'.

A lifeboat station opened at Grange Chine in 1860, continuing in operation till 1915. During the Napoleonic Wars there was a barracks built for 50 soldiers and there are tales of the garrison pickled on smuggled brandy. During the Second World War concrete fortifications were erected against enemy landings. The bridge (more properly a viaduct) that carries the Military Road across the chine was built in the 1860s with bricks made on site.

Chilton Chine (*chil*, chalk and *ton*, settlement) is a shallow trough; below the chine stretches Bull Face Ledge, another notorious reef and perhaps referred to in an Anglo Saxon document of AD 826 as *bican doene* or 'the bitch's mouth'. Just west of the chine a total of 26 dinosaur footprints was found in 1977. Three Salter children drowned here whilst gathering winkles in 1913.

Venables calls Brook Chine 'a mere open watercourse sunk in the green sward, quite devoid of beauty'. On the adjacent green is the roofless Lifeboat House. Between Brook Chine and Hanover Point a new chine is gradually forming and is called by some Churchill Chine.

Shippards Chine was formerly known as Compton Grange Chine, the grange being one of the many granaries once belonging to Quarr Abbey. The chine is now a popular place for surfers to access the swells that roll in from the Atlantic. The last of the chines along this coastline is Compton Chine, a narrow fissure in the clifftop.

The only way down to the beach at Alum Bay is through the chine. From the late eighteenth century tourists began to arrive to see the coloured sands. After the pier was built Alfred Isaacs, piermaster, ran a café selling water at 1d a glass to the growing numbers of visitors. Despite subsidence a footpath still runs through the chine beneath a chairlift which is now one of the island's chief tourist attractions. The remaining chines (Widdick, Colwell, Brambles and Linstone) have little of interest.

'Where Tritons come to meditate'

If you had visited Freshwater Bay in the mid-nineteenth century you would have encountered one of many boatmen who would doubtless have pressed into your hand a card of the wonders to be seen between Freshwater Bay and Alum Bay, numbered one to fifteen. These wonders could only be appreciated from the water and a boat trip to Alum Bay and back would cost you 10/- in 1879.

Walls of perpendicular white chalk have been sculpted by the waves into caverns where, according to one impressionable writer, 'sea monsters might retire to sleep or Tritons come to meditate'. There are ledges and arches, rocks and pillars all with fantastic names, some with tales real and imagined. So let's take a boat trip beneath these 'mural precipices', after first taking in the delights of the Bay itself.

On the eastern side of Freshwater Bay are sea stacks, among them the remains of *Arched Rock* whose arch finally gave way on 25 October 1992. The westernmost rock is *Deer Bound Rock* or *Stag Rock*; a local tale tells of a hard-pressed deer that leaped from the cliff to the patch of grass at its summit to escape Lord Holmes' baying hounds. A third sea stack, called the

Arch Rock and Stag Rock, with Freshwater Cliffs in the background, in 1840.

Mermaid Rock, is the most recent, having become detached from the cliff in 1969. The western side of Freshwater Bay is a honeycomb of caves, the most famous being *Freshwater Cavern (1)*. The cavern was 120 feet deep until the roof collapsed in the 1850s and what was left was shored up to withstand the firing of the guns in the battery above.

Round the corner to the west are the four dark mouthed *caverns (2)* of *Watcombe Bay* and *Picturesque Rock (3)* which, according to Venables, was 'a grotesque pyramidal mass of chalk . . . rising boldly from the water'. It rises boldly no more having succumbed to the sea. In quick succession are *Neptune's Caves (4)*, the larger 200 feet deep, the smaller 90 feet deep, and *Bar Cave (5)* – also 90 feet deep. The boatmen would sometimes fire a pistol in the caves to prove the loudness of the echo.

Further west is the The Nodes, the highest point on the cliffs of Tennyson Down and where the beacon warning of invasion was once sited. In 1892, following the poet's death, it was replaced by the Tennyson Memorial Cross, which is now maintained by Trinity House as a sea-mark. Round *New Ditch Point* lies *Frenchman's Hole (6)*, where a poor French prisoner who escaped confinement hid and starved to death:

Day after day,
Sad at the gloomy cavern's mouth he sat,
And viewed the main that ever toiled beneath;
Still fondly forming in the farthest verge,
Where the round ether mixes with the waves,
Ships dim discovered, dropping from the clouds;
At evening to the setting sun he turned
A mournful eye, and down his dying heart
Sunk hopeless.
(from Hargrove's *Wanderings in the Isle of Wight*)

The next three caves take their name from *Lord Holmes (7)*, Governor of the island in 1763/4. His lordship was given to entertaining his friends in the caves; his wine was cooled in *Lord Holmes Cellar*, food prepared in *Lord Holmes Kitchen* and the entertaining took place in *Lord Holmes Parlour*.

Wedge Rock (8) was a triangular fragment of chalk lodged between the main cliff and an isolated pyramid about 50 feet high. Above it was *Roe's Hall (8)* and the green or ledge said to be the only haunt of the Isle of Wight Wave moth. Past a detached lump of chalk still known as *Old Pepper Rock (9)* is the sheer perpendicularity of *Main Bench (10)*. Here between *Old*

When the 120-foot pinnacle of rock known as Lot's Wife fell into the sea in 1764
the crash was heard in Portsmouth.

Pepper Rock and *Sun Corner*, a stern wave-worn bluff at the western end of
Main Bench, lies the main seabird breeding colony which, says Worsley, once
included 'puffins, razorbills, willocks, gulls, cormorants, Cornish choughs,
daws, starlings and wild pigeons'. *Prestons Bower (11)* was another cave
above the beach in the cliff.

Round *Sun Corner* lies *Scratchell's Bay (12)* and the magnificent *Grand
Arch*. Geologist Gideon Mantell wrote 'In the face of the cliff, from the
destruction of the lower beds of the bent strata, a magnificent arch 300 feet
high has been produced, and forms an alcove that overhangs the beach 150
feet'. It was once known as *St Christopher's Cliffs*, behind which on the
downs was the original lighthouse and a signal station. Just inside the bay the
waves have tunnelled a low gloomy cavern known as *Needles Cave (13)*
which runs as much as 300 feet into the cliff. At the northern end are the Isle
of Wight's most famous landmark, the *Needles Rocks (14)* – three wedge-
shaped sea stacks. They were named after a fourth needle-shaped rock
between the second and third stack. This rock was a slender conical pinnacle
120 feet high known as *Lot's Wife* which fell in 1764, supposedly with a
crash whose shockwaves were felt in Portsmouth. The stump is still visible at
low water.

Off the south end of *Scratchell's Bay* is *St Anthony's Rock*. It is possible
the rock acquired it's name from the ship *St Anthony*, which was lost here in
1691. Off the northern end of the Needles lies the notorious *Goose Rock*,
which has claimed two naval warships under identical circumstances.

Past the *Needles* and you enter *Alum Bay (15)*; 'one side of it a wall of
glowing chalk, the other a barrier of rainbows' according to one guidebook.
At the southern end of Alum Bay is a watery cavern in the chalk known as
Mother Large's Kitchen. Further north a small spring trickling from a fissure

Culver Cliff, at the eastern end of the island.

in the chalk is known as *Mother Large's Well*. The coloured sands, in 21 recognised shades, are rightly famous; 'the tints of the cliffs are so bright and so varied, that they have not the aspect of anything natural. Deep purplish red, dusky blue, bright ochreous yellow, grey very nearly approaching to white, and absolute black, succeed each other as sharply defined as the stripes in silk'. (Englefield) The traditional way up and down to the pebbly beach is by the path through *Alum Bay Chine* but since April 1973 a chairlift offers a more leisurely and panoramic route down the cliffs.

Culver Cliffs

The precipitous chalk bulwark of Culver Cliffs is the eastern reflection of the chalk bluffs of Freshwater, and indeed the same beds of rock outcrop at Whitecliff Bay that furnish the coloured sands of Alum Bay. It was on the crags of Culver that the young poet Algernon Swinburne felt compelled to test his courage following his father's refusal to allow him to join the army.

Believing wrongly that his father considered he lacked nerve he clambered up the white face of Culver not once but twice in the cold of winter to gain the top and thus prove, at least to himself, that he wasn't a coward.

The name Culver is derived from the Anglo-Saxon *culfre* meaning dove or pigeon, which were once numerous here. So too were hawks which were protected under Queen Elizabeth I, possibly in a royal preserve. In 1564 she issued a warrant for the Captain of the Island to search for thieves who were stealing these hawks. Today it is the peregrine falcon you are more likely to see from the slopes of Culver Down or the hovering kestrel. Culver Cliffs are the principal seabird nesting site at the eastern end of the island and the haunt of the solitary raven.

Thirty feet below the top of the cliff was a cave known as the Hermit's Hole, which could be approached by a precipitous pathway from the down. Folklore tells of an ogre living there who used to bludgeon his victims with a club. In the fourteenth century the hermit's warnings of invasion went unheeded, leading to the burning and dissolution of Wolverton near Brading. Round the corner in Whitecliff Bay smugglers landing contraband hauled their goods up the cliff by block and tackle till an accident lead to the death of a local inhabitant. In the Bay itself brown coal was worked from a trench on the beach, but it's fumey brimstone smell was not popular. The tide still uncovers the occasional trench prop.

On a low spring tide it is possible to walk from Whitecliff Bay round the nose of Culver Cliff on a layered wave-cut platform. Dwarfed beneath perpendicular walls Culver seems even more imposing and grand. Horseshoe Bay is a tiny cove full of grey stones and pebbles; one arm of the cove is formed by the jutting promontory of the White Horse, sometimes known as the Anvil. Scramble round this and you encounter the twin caves of the Nostrils. Beneath the south face of Culver at low tide you may be able to see the rusted skeleton of the tug *Harry Sharman,* which ran aground here in 1970 while fighting the fire on the *Pacific Glory* and helped contain the oilslick.

Gulls, guillemots and gannets

Inaccessible ledges on the near vertical faces of sheer chalk cliffs provide ideal nest sites for many seabirds. At Culver Cliff cormorants, shags, herring gulls and great black-backed gulls breed in small numbers. They breed in greater numbers on Highdown Cliffs and Main Bench alongside guillemots, razorbills and fulmars. The best way to see them is by getting in close under the cliffs in a boat.

On a boat trip beneath Main Bench at Freshwater C.J. Cornish described how the 'puffins, razorbills and guillemots . . . look like strings of little black and white beads stretched row below row across the chalk'. The birds 'sit on their lofty ledges . . . unconcerned until the visitor rows in close to the cliff. Then the whole concourse groan in chorus like a well drilled political meeting . . . On the water the razorbills and puffins are so tame that they will let the boat within a dozen yards of them. The razorbills swim with their beaks tilted upwards and their tails low in the water, which gives them a saucy independent air, quite unlike that of any other bird'. Since Cornish's time the puffins no longer breed and razorbills have dwindled to a few pairs, but there are still plenty of guillemots, cormorants and now fulmars.

Seabirds are safe on sheer cliffs from all but one predator – man. Before legislation was passed to protect wildlife everything was considered fair game. In Victorian times shooting parties would set out in boats intent on finding amusing sport amongst the birds at Culver Cliff or the Needles. Locals known as cliffmen would lower themselves on ropes over the cliff edge in search of eggs to sell to visitors. Naturalists were also collectors of specimens and ready with a gun. In April 1844 the Rev Charles Bury, a regular contributor to the *Zoologist* and an expert on birds, was delighted to be able to shoot a hoopoe for his collection. Today happily such uncommon visitors can expect only to be shot on film!

Two majestic birds have found the remoteness and inaccessibility they crave on the coastal cliffs of the south coast – the raven and the peregrine falcon. Fred Mew, in his book *Back of the Wight,* recalls sitting on the clifftop at Blackgang in 1913 watching both, and that same spot is a good place to see these solitary birds today.

Walk along the sea wall between Shanklin and Sandown and you are likely to encounter one of the island's success stories – the fulmar. It's stiff-winged flight and ceaseless chattering are unmistakeable. It nests in holes in the cliff, returning each year to the same nest with the same mate. They have slowly spread from Icelandic stock southwards and there are now many colonies along the island's south coast.

Their phenomenal success is surprising in view of the fulmar's slow breeding rate. They only lay one egg, which is not replaced if lost to a predator, and the adolescent fulmar won't breed till eight years old! This is perhaps compensated by a remarkably long life, some birds surviving more than 30 years. The fulmar's gradual spread south is thought to be due to the availability of abundant supplies of offal from whalers. There is no whaling anymore but modern fishing (with the catch gutted at sea) has taken its place as its primary food source.

If you go to the southern tip of the island, St Catherine's Point, at dawn during the eight weeks from March to May you are likely to witness the spring passage of birds flying west to east. The nineteenth century poet Sidney Dobell, wintering on the Undercliff, tells how 'a week ago there passed, every morning for an hour, at a distance of about half a mile from shore, innumerable armies, all flying west to east. Most of them dark, but officered by large white gulls with black tips to the wings. The rank and file flew in companies of ten to fifteen, but the succession of such companies was bewildering'. Some days the passage of birds is unforgettable, with divers, gulls, terns, skuas, gannets, guillemots, shearwaters, ducks and waders.

Newtown National Nature Reserve is the largest and most important of the island's estuaries and has avoided the intrusive development typical of other south coast habitats. Because of this it is an important over-wintering and feeding ground for wildfowl and waders. In winter there are large flocks of brent and Canada geese, as well as hundreds of golden plovers and other small waders. One of the delights of Newtown is watching flocks of dunlin wheel and turn in flight, their wings flashing white as they catch the light. The peregrine causes a stir when it makes a visit and an osprey is a brief visitor in September. Newtown contains the only nesting colony of the black-headed gull in the island.

Life at the sea's edge

The seashore is the meeting place of two very different elements. Sea and land overlap in a marginal world that is forever changing. The shore has a dual nature, and life within it has a foot in two camps. It is the rhythm of the tides that dictates when life belongs to the sea and when to the land. Only the most hardy and adaptable can survive the cycle of submersion and exposure twice daily.

When the tide recedes life is exposed to great differences in temperature, from hot sun to frost and risk of dessication by drying winds; on the other hand there is abundant light for marine plants like seaweeds. When the tide returns it brings with it a steady supply of food and oxygen. Rough weather and breaking waves batter mercilessly and can pluck plants from their anchorage; a rainstorm can change the salinity of water in the shallows.

Rocky shores in this inter-tidal zone are dominated by the seaweeds. Nearly 300 species of seaweed are found around the island's coast and the best place to find them is on Bembridge Ledge. Tough leathery brown seaweeds dominate the middle shore; when the tide is out they lie flat, a heavy curtain of sodden rubbery fronds that holds moisture and beneath which nothing ever dries out. Green seaweeds are more likely further up the beach and smaller red seaweeds are commonest in rockpools.

Abundant everywhere is the common limpet, which clamps itself tightly to a rock to resist drying out. When covered with seawater the limpet unclamps itself and walks over to its garden of algae and begins to feed; as the tide recedes it returns to the exact same spot where it's irregular edges are sure of a snug fit! Barnacles also clamp themselves to rocks, but instead of moving they open a door to catch food when the tide is in and close it tight when it's out.

Island shores are rich in sea-anemones. Anemones have tentacles which release disabling darts into small creatures unlucky enough to brush past; the prey is then shovelled into its mouth. The common beadlet anemone contracts to a green or red blob of jelly when the tide is out and produces a sticky substance to stop it drying up.

Molluscs with a single rounded shell simply withdraw into their shell and allow the sea to knock them about. There are top shells, so-called because they resemble spinning tops, and dog whelks that spend their time sucking on barnacles or trepanning into mussels. The small periwinkle has had enough of this double life and has almost completed the transition to land by acquiring lungs! Bivalves like mussels and clams withdraw their feeding tube and sit tight. Then there are those that hide by burrowing into sand, crawling into crevices and under rocks or, like the extraordinary piddock, living imprisoned in rock in a bore-hole of it's own making.

In estuaries plants that inhabit the saltmarsh have to tolerate salt around their roots, twice daily flooding and drying winds. Seablite not only tolerates but loves the salt water. Another halophyte (or 'salt lover') is marsh samphire which, like seablite, brings a splash of red to Newtown in autumn. Other plants of the saltmarsh are the purple-flowering sea lavender and thrift or sea pink.

In some areas of saltmarsh there is a dense growth of grass which has a remarkable history. Over 100 years ago the native small cord-grass was a rare plant growing in a few salt marshes. Even rarer was American cord-grass, which was probably introduced by shipping in about 1829. In 1870 James Groves found a third kind which he named Townsend's cord-grass. It turned out to be a cross between the other two and much more vigorous, spreading rapidly. Then in 1892 yet another grass was found, a result of Townsend's cord-grass doubling its chromosomes to create a new species called common cord-grass which is now dominant throughout the Solent. It is remarkable to realise that a new species has evolved within living memory by a process which is responsible for many present day species, but whose origin is lost in the distant evolutionary past.

SAVING LIVES

Wrecks, Lights and Lifeboats

OVER THE centuries thousands of ships have come to grief along the shores of the Isle of Wight, and 'wreck' was once a major source of income. Parish boundaries were distorted to ensure a slice of shoreline and there were intimations of deliberate wrecking. An old law stated that the owner of a wrecked vessel could only recover salvaged goods provided one member of its crew survived. How often was a helping hand withheld by islanders with their eyes on the cargo? In 1224 the Bishop of Winchester decreed the excommunication of any man guilty of failing to help the shipwrecked and this threat was ordered to be read three times a year in island churches. To those making a precarious living from fishing and farm work the harvest of the sea was a welcome addition to their income, either in the form of goods washed up and spirited away or from work on salvaging ship and cargo. In the nineteenth century those same folk who accepted the bounty of the sea were ready to risk their lives manning the lifeboats.

A sailing ship heading up Channel or bound for Portsmouth or Southampton the long way round was safe so long as it stood well out to sea. But in the inky blackness of a storm and unable to fix it's position accurately a sailing ship could get into trouble and become 'embayed'. A light almost anywhere along the south coast would be enough to save all but the most foolhardy, the negligent or the unlucky. The Back of the Wight with it's treacherous ledges, lack of shelter and exposure to Atlantic swells is the graveyard of many ships caught on a lee shore by a south westerly gale and unable to make it round Rocken End. With justification the *Times* once called Chale Bay, 'the Receiver General of Wrecks for the Isle of Wight.'

The Pepperpot and Mustard Pot

In 1313 the *St Mary of Bayonne* sailed from Gascony with a cargo of wine bound for the Monastery of Livers in Picardy. In late April she was driven

The Island's first lighthouse built in 1328 by
Walter de Godeton of Chale as a penance.

ashore in Chale Bay. The crew survived and saved most of the cargo, which
they sold off to locals. Among the buyers was Walter de Godeton of Chale
who bought 53 barrels from the crew. Gascony belonged to the English
Crown and the ship's owners sought justice through the English courts. De
Godeton was found guilty of illegally receiving goods and fined 267 marks,
a large sum in those days.

That was not all. The Pope charged him with sacrilege and threatened
Walter with excommunication unless he built a lighthouse on St Catherine's
Hill and a chantry for a priest to say prayers for the souls of those lost at sea.
The lighthouse was finished in 1328 and dedicated to St Catherine. The light
was maintained until the Dissolution in the 1530s when the chantry was
suppressed. The tower remained as a sea mark, and in the eighteenth century
Richard Worsley had buttresses added to save it from falling down – thus
making it look much like an early rocket. Today it is the second oldest
surviving lighthouse in Britain.

As a lighthouse it was never very effective, and was often wreathed in low

The lighthouse on Freshwater Cliffs, built in 1785, proved ineffective because of sea mists.

cloud or fog. In 1785 a new lighthouse was started but never completed, again because of fog on the downs. The original lighthouse is known as 'the Pepperpot' and the newer incomplete one 'the Mustard Pot'.

St Catherine's Lighthouse

The spur to action is often tragedy and the incentive for a lighthouse came from the loss of the *Clarendon*. The West Indiaman left St Kitts in August 1836 with a cargo of sugar, molasses and rum. On board were Captain Walker and a crew of sixteen plus ten passengers, including five young girls. On the morning of 11 October she became embayed in a gale and drove ashore at Blackgang. Within five minutes the ship broke up in the huge waves. Ex-navy man John Wheeler watched the stricken vessel and helped to rescue the second mate and two seamen but the rest perished, crushed by the ship's timbers.

The victim's terrified cries for help and the battered bodies of the five girls left the inhabitants of Chale shocked and horrified. The demand for a lighthouse became a clamour and Trinity House was stung into action. A 120

The original lighthouse at St Catherine's (left) was 120 feet high and began shining in 1840. In 1875 the lighthouse was lowered (right) to just 86 feet high after problems with fog.

foot tower was built at Rocken End on a base 72 feet above the sea and began shining in March 1840. In 1875, following problems with fog and low cloud, the tower was lowered to its present height of 86 feet. The light is one of the brightest on the British coast and can be seen in France on a clear night. In 1943 the light was put out of operation by an air raid which claimed the lives of the three lighthouse keepers.

The Needles Lighthouse

In 1781, following a number of recent shipwrecks, a group of London merchants lobbied Trinity House in favour of a lighthouse at the Needles. In 1785 a low squat cone-shaped building was erected on the summit known as St Christopher's, at a height of 474 ft above the sea. The light consisted of 10 lamps and the same number of plated reflectors and consumed 700 gallons of oil a year.

It began operation in September 1786, the keeper and his family living in adjoining buildings. Sir H.C. Englefield wrote in 1816, 'in hard blowing weather the fury of the wind on this promontory is scarce credible. Very large flints and fragments of chalk are blown from the cliffs so as to endanger the windows of the lighthouse, and for many days in succession it is scarcely possible to open the door'. In November 1832 the keeper, Thomas Colereine, fell to his death from Highdown Cliff into the sea amidst rumours that he was murdered by smugglers, leaving his widow to tend the light.

As with St Catherine's so also with St Christopher's. The lighthouse was often shrouded in mist and it was replaced in 1859 by a new one at the end of the Needles rocks. In a plan devised by architect James Walker the furthermost stack was dynamited to create a platform for a 109 foot high circular granite tower with walls a yard thick at the base and 1fi feet thick at the top. During winter the crew of three were likely to be cut off for weeks and so the lighthouse was supplied with a 2,400 gallon water tank whilst a coal store was blasted out of the stack.

Living in close confinement must have put a strain on the men. Tony Isaacs, who delivered the papers and other supplies, recalled one keeper being taken off following an argument over a cricket match. Following the laying of an electric cable out to the lighthouse to replace the generator, it was fully automated in 1994, thus ending 208 years of manned lighthouse-keeping at the Needles.

The Lifeboat Arrives

Henry Greathead developed the first true lifeboat towards the end of the eighteenth century. In 1824 the National Institution for the Preservation of Life from Shipwreck was founded, later to be re-formed into the Royal National Lifeboat Institution. Before the first lifeboat stations were established on the island in 1860 the coastguards took a more active role in rescues. Formed in 1822 to police the coast and combat smuggling they found themselves increasingly called upon to save lives. They were aided by a rocket apparatus devised by John Dennett, a Newport man. His working prototype could fire a line up to 250 yards. The device was stationed with the coastguards at Atherfield and when the 430-ton *Bainsbridge* went aground on the ledge in October 1832 it was successfully used to get a line to the ship, enabling the coastguards to haul a boat out to the stricken vessel and take off all 19 of its crew.

In the winter of 1859 the Maltese barque, the *Mirabata*, loaded with oats, broke up on Brighstone Ledge with the loss of 11 of her 16 crew. On the same day the schooner *Sentinel*, of Caernarfon, came ashore at Brook and two of the crew were swept away. The loss of life following these shipwrecks prompted the coastguards and others at the inquest to state that if a lifeboat had been to hand those lives may have been saved. The Rev Pellew Gaze of Brook, who had taken an active part in the attempted rescue, and his

The first Rescue at Grange Chine in August 1860. The Rev E. McCall (in top hat) and the Rev John Pellew Gaze (second from the right) were instrumental in raising the money for the first lifeboats.

colleague from Brighstone, the Rev McCall, wrote to the RNLI. The result was a recommendation for two lifeboats, one at Brook and the other at Grange Chine.

At the same time as the two rectors launched their appeal for funds the Royal Victoria Yacht Club was doing the same independently. Together they raised enough money for the two boats, boathouses and running costs for a year. Both stations were opened in August 1860. Brighstone's boat was named *Rescue* and Brook's boat was called *Dauntless*. From 1891 a third lifeboat, the *Catherine Swift*, was stationed at Atherfield. Brook's crews were to save 263 lives and Brighstone's crews 433 lives. Despite having to be lowered 240 feet down steep crumbling cliffs, Atherfield's boat went on to rescue 157 souls.

The launching of the Brook and Brighstone's boats was a spectacular affair, involving up to 60 helpers as well as a crew of ten picked oarsmen and a team of eight heavy horses to pull the boat. The call-out began with a maroon being fired to summon the crew and the beach handling party. The boat would be hauled to the beach, driven into the sea and turned bow first with the crew aboard. The critical part was the timing of the launch off the carriage, and that depended on the skill and experience of the coxswain.

Jack Seely, later the first Lord Mottistone, was a member of the crew under coxswain Ben Jacobs and in his book *Adventure* recalls the moment of launch. 'At last the coxswain chose the right moment; after a great wave had nearly lifted us off the carriage, he raised his right hand above his head and roared out 'Launch'. There was a rumbling sound as the boat ran over the rollers on her way to the sea and, with a crash, into the water we went. How we pulled, my God, how we pulled! Every man knew that it was our only chance to get enough way on the boat to surmount the next wave. Then it came. We could hear it roaring, though we dared not look round, for we had to devote our whole mind and strength to pulling. Up went the bow, up, up, until the boat was nearly perpendicular, but over the crest she went and for a moment we were safe'.

The launch was a daunting affair, more so on a pitch black night with gale force winds drowning human voices and everyone soaked to the skin. The boat could be required to make several journeys and be afloat for hours. It required enormous strength and iron determination amongst the crew for a successful rescue, a fact recognised by the many decorations awarded the island crews by the RNLI.

In 1868 the *City of Worcester* was delivered to the new RNLI lifeboat station at Bembridge and the following year another independent station was established at Ryde. In 1869 the *Dove* came to Totland Bay, money for the boat being raised by the IW Sunday School Committee. When the RNLI took over Totland in 1885 the *Dove* was moved to a new station at Shanklin where it stayed until washed away in 1917. By the early 1900s major shipwrecks were becoming rarer and there was less to do for the lifeboats. Brighstone and Atherfield stations were disbanded in 1915. In 1924 two new motor lifeboats at Bembridge and Yarmouth with their greater range and speed took over most of the work, though Brook stayed in operation until 1937.

In November 2000 the Yarmouth Lifeboat Station took delivery of the *Eric and Susan Hiscock*, a 57 foot long, 40-ton 'Seven' class lifeboat capable of 25 knots. Her arrival was not without incident; en route she was diverted to attend a disabled car-carrier in the English Channel. A crew of seven includes a full-time coxswain and mechanic. Bembridge has the *Max Aitken*

III, a 1987 'Tyne' class lifeboat, 47 feet long and with a maximum speed of 18 knots. The boat is slipway launched from the end of a pier and requires a shore recovery gang. In 2003 the Bembridge station received 40 call-outs and the Yarmouth station 35.

'A chance too good to be missed'

An extraordinary variety of cargoes from all over the world have sailed up the Back of the Wight. Beans and barley from Egypt, rum and sugar from Demarara, gum from New Zealand, grain, oil and feathers from Russia and cotton from New Orleans have all been salvaged or stolen (in most cases both) from ships that have foundered along this stretch of coast. In Fred Mew's words wrecks 'helped to fill many larders and empty tummies'.

The owner of shipwrecked goods had the right to recover them and anybody who removed goods from the scene of a wreck was guilty of theft and subject to the law. This didn't stop crowds of islanders appearing at wrecks and spiriting away what the tide had brought in. It was the coastguards' duty to police the coasts and protect shipwrecked goods. In practice they were often overwhelmed by sheer numbers and turned a blind eye; on occasions they even joined in the bonanza. Nevertheless some islanders did find themselves in court.

One wreck, fondly remembered as the 'flour' ship, was the steamship *Wheatfield* which came ashore at Blackgang in 1882. Bags of flour and tins of beef began to disappear and police and coastguard were kept busy – though they were not averse to the odd tin themselves! The previous year the *Alpheus Marshall* delivered up 14lb tins of beef, tinned prawns and tomatoes to the people of Chale. When the steam trawler *Nemrod* foundered at Walpen Chine in 1910 she spilled part of her cargo of 70 tons of fish. Cod, haddock, gurnet, plaice, sole and turbot were washed ashore, along with the baskets used for handling the catch. 'The frying pans in the neighbourhood rarely had such a busy time', observed Fred Mew.

In 1918 the *War Knight* provided the war-rationed inhabitants of Freshwater with a welcome harvest of bacon, lard and flour. Wagons, prams and bikes carted off whole sides of bacon and 28lb boxes of lard. Fred Mew, who was stationed there, saw 'parts of pigs going in all directions'. Thirty eight people were summonsed and the train which took them to court in Newport was called 'the Bacon and Lard Special'.

Spirits is one cargo guaranteed to cause chaos. The *Lotus* was wrecked at Blackgang in 1862 and disgorged a cargo of rum. The papers were full of accusations of drunkenness among the crowd on the beach and even among the rescue services, overshadowing the tragic fact that only two of the fourteen people on board survived. The *Russe* went ashore in 1902 bringing the lucky locals a feast of bloaters, lard, butter, sausages and pork. In addition casks of wines and spirits were strewn along the beach and the crowd carried off what they could in buckets and jars; those without containers drank what they could there and then until the authorities broke open the casks and poured the contents into the sea.

Perhaps the most surprising cargo to reach these shores was aboard the *Cedarine*, which struck Brighstone Ledge in April 1862. She was carrying 191 convicts returning from Bermuda having finished their sentences. They were all saved, including a further 43 passengers and crew, by the Brighstone lifeboat on it's first call out. The convicts made their way to Brighstone, drank both pubs dry and started brawling in the street. Order was only restored when troops from Parkhurst arrived.

If a wreck couldn't bring food or materials into the household it often brought the next best thing – work. The Scottish steamer *Cormorant* left New Orleans with a cargo of raw cotton and beached at Whale Chine in December 1886. Attempts to refloat her failed and men and carriers from all over the island were hired to unload the cotton bales. The wreck was sold and broken up, providing work for several years. Fred Mew said 'she brought more money into the place than any wreck before or since'.

Miracles and Disasters

The *Eider* has gold, she has human lives;
But these can assist no more
Pray, pray, ye German children and wives
For help from the English shore!

The German luxury liner the *Eider* struck Atherfield Ledge in thick fog on a January evening in 1892. As she did so the fog cleared and onlookers were surprised and dumbfounded by the most spectacular sight. 'It looked like a town on the rocks', some said. The brilliantly lit ship was a four masted, twin funnelled, single screw steamer of 4,719 tons over 430 feet long. She carried

The German luxury liner *SS Eider*. As well as passengers and crew the lifeboats took off eight and a half tons of gold and silver worth £300,000.

167 crew, 227 passengers, 500 sacks of mail and £300,000 worth of gold and silver ingots.

Captain Hienecke refused an offer of help from the Atherfield lifeboat believing his ship would float off at the next high tide and asked for tugs to attend. The tugs couldn't get close enough and by 10 am next morning, with the storm worsening, Captain Hienecke decided to evacuate the passengers. The three lifeboats stationed along the Back of the Wight worked through the day to rescue all the passengers, making a total of 18 dangerous trips. The following day they made a further 11 trips to take off the crew and all the mailbags. After accepting an offer of reward money, the crews made another 12 trips to bring ashore the gold and silver, the ship's silver plate and the passengers' luggage – earning themselves a total of £543.

The *Eider* was the biggest shipwreck to date and because the rescue was so conspicuously successful it attracted huge public interest. Among the visitors to the rescue scene was H.R.H. Prince Henry of Battenberg, Governor of the I.W., and the Prince of Wales accompanied by Prince George (the future George V). Queen Victoria conveyed her 'warm appreciation of the gallant conduct displayed by the crews' and James Cotton, coxswain of

The wreck of the *Irex* in Scratchell's Bay in 1890.

the Grange lifeboat, was awarded the silver medal of the RNLI. The coxswains of all three boats received gold watches from the German Kaiser bearing his portrait and a personal inscription.

Another miraculous rescue was that of the *Irex*, the biggest sailing ship to be wrecked on the island's coast. She was on her maiden voyage and went aground in Scratchells Bay in January 1890. It's an extraordinary tale involving a demented captain, accusations of cowardice among the lifeboat crew and a record-breaking rocket launch.

The ship was bound for Rio de Janeiro but since leaving the Clyde had experienced nothing but gale force winds. Capt Hutton had little sleep for 24 days and had begun to lose his senses, refusing the crew's request to seek a sheltered port to put ashore two injured seamen. Eventually Hutton turned round in the Bay of Biscay and ran for Falmouth, but could engage no pilot. The ship then headed up Channel in the storm and Hutton 'behaved like a madman', mistaking the Needles light for a pilot boat, with the result that the *Irex* went aground beneath the tall cliffs of Scratchells Bay.

In the struggle to free the ship's lifeboats the captain and first mate were swept overboard. The crew climbed the rigging to escape the heavy seas breaking over the decks. The Totland lifeboat was called out at 10 am next morning and was towed by the collier *Hampshire* to within sight of the wreck. As they rowed closer there was dissent amongst the crew; some feared conditions were beyond them, others were willing to risk all. To the great surprise of the crowd of onlookers now gathered at the clifftop, the coxswain turned back. In the days that followed a verbal storm broke over the behaviour of the lifeboat crews. Accusations of cowardice were bandied about, and within a year the coxswain had been replaced.

Hopes now rested on a cliff rescue using the rocket apparatus. Coastguard Hallett's first shot hit the rigging. It took two hours for the crew to secure the hawser but at 3pm the first seaman was hauled to safety. It was exhausting work and the coastguards were helped by volunteers and a detachment of troops from Golden Hill Fort. By midnight all the surviving crew had been hauled ashore except one poor lad named Jones who was afraid to abandon his refuge clinging to the mast. He spent the night lashed to it for his own safety. In the morning Isaac Rose, a black seaman, and coastguard Machin went back for the boy, who they found 'blue with cold and half dead'. Jones survived, bringing the total saved to 29 out of the 36 on board.

The three-masted *Sirenia* came to grief on Atherfield Ledge in March 1888. The captain refused an offer from a pilot cutter to take off everyone aboard, hoping to refloat on the next tide. But in the huge breaking seas the ship was at grave risk and the Brighstone lifeboat was launched. The women and children were taken off. Later, with the weather worsening, they made a second trip and whilst returning to the beach the lifeboat was capsized and four men were lost – two from the *Sirenia*, along with Moses Munt, the coxswain, and Thomas Cotton, the second coxswain of the Brighstone lifeboat.

Hopes for the crew of the *Sirenia* still on board rested with the Brook lifeboat. After battling for fifteen hours and losing second coxswain Reuben Cooper they were forced back to Brook. A second crew was raised for the Brighstone boat and the remaining thirteen men successfully rescued. All but two of the thirty one aboard the *Sirenia* were saved at the cost of the tragic loss of three brave local men.

Naval Catastrophes

Some of the worst catastrophes in the waters around the Isle of Wight have involved ships of the Royal Navy. The incompetence of her officers and the negligence of the Navy Board have both been blamed for the loss of the *Royal George* in 1782. Certainly, it could have been avoided. The exact death toll is unknown for the ship was crowded with well-wishers as well as the 821 crew. Bodies were washed ashore at Ryde for weeks and hastily buried near the shore, only to be unearthed by developers in the 1840s. A memorial stone was erected in Ashley Gardens in 1965.

HMS Assurance, under the command of Patterson, the ship's master, was negotiating the Needles Channel in April 1752. She was bringing home the retiring Governor of Jamaica. As the white stacks of the Needles loomed the governor asked how close they would get. Patterson replied 'so close that the fly of the ensign might touch the rock'. How embarrassed he must have felt when the ship became impaled on Goose Rock, a stone's throw from the outermost stack. Though the ship was a wreck the governor managed to salvage most of the £60,000 fortune he had brought back with him, but he died the following year. Patterson spent three months in a debtor's jail.

The 38-gun frigate *Pomone* was returning from service in the Mediterranean in 1811 when she foundered in identical circumstances. On board was Sir Harford Jones, the British ambassador to Persia, who had secret intelligence regarding the war with France. Also on board were some Persian horses, a present from the Shah to George III. The ship was a wreck but much was saved including the horses, offloaded through a gunport. The ship's master was severely reprimanded for the ship's loss at the ensuing Court Martial. Ironically, the *Pomone* settled on the remains of the *Assurance*.

The sail-training ship *Eurydice* was lost in a sudden squall off Dunnose Point in March 1878. She was returning from a tour of the West Indies with 366 aboard, under full sail and with her gun ports open. There were two other boats in the area – a fishing boat and the schooner *Emma*. On seeing the approaching squall the fishing boat pulled in close to shore and the *Emma* shortened sail. But the *Eurydice* took no action till it was too late and she was laid over till her gun ports took in water and she sank. There were only two survivors – Sidney Fletcher and Benjamin Cuddiford.

Both the inquest and Court Martial attached no blame to the officers and

HMS Eurydice was knocked flat in a sudden snow squall off
Dunnose Point in March 1878.

crew but came up with no explanation either. Did St Boniface Down hide the
squall from the ship till the last moment? Or do we believe Sidney Fletcher
who, years later, told his family the whole ship's company were drunk and
that, relaxed through too much rum, they were simply caught off guard?

In April 1908, *HMS Gladiator*, a second class fleet cruiser, was steaming
up the Needles Channel in a snow squall when the bow of the 11,630-ton
liner *St Paul* appeared out of the blizzard heading straight for her. When on
a collision course ships are required to alter direction to starboard in order
to pass each other on the port side. Inexplicably, the *Gladiator* did the
opposite and the liner ploughed into her. When the liner had disengaged, the
Gladiator was driven ashore by the wind at Sconce Point near Yarmouth.

By this time many of the crew were in the cold sea. As soon as they realised
what was happening, men of the Royal Engineers stationed at Fort Victoria
launched hastily found boats or waded and swam to the rescue. Altogether,
one officer and 27 crew drowned, mostly trapped below as the ship turned
over.

At the inquest, Lumsden, the *Gladiator's* captain as good as admitted confusion over the *St Paul's* signals and turning his ship to port. But before he could incriminate himself further he invoked his right to refuse to give evidence. Lumsden faced a court martial over the loss of his ship but the worst he received was a reprimand.

POLICING THE COAST

The War against Smuggling

CHARLES LAMB once said, 'I like a smuggler, he's the only honest thief'. The high import duties that made smuggling a lucrative business were loathed by everyone and so-called free-traders had the sympathy if not the respect of the majority of islanders. It was said that eight out of ten islanders were involved, either as active smugglers or knowing consumers of contraband, including many respected pillars of the community. Tales of canny island folk outwitting the Preventive men were no doubt exaggerated and tend to gloss over the darker side of smuggling. The threat of violence to avoid arrest was ever present, for the penalties on conviction could be harsh.

Smuggling paid well and farm labourers and fishermen on low wages and intermittent employment were glad of the money. This was often put into bricks and mortar; in the parish of Chale lots of farm workers owned their own houses and many a row of Bembridge cottages was paid for by smuggling. A visitor to Niton was struck by fishermen who never seemed to go fishing but always had plenty of money to spend. Idleness and drunkenness were common among the smuggling gangs. One observer noted a 'lawless spirit'. Men with time on their hands and access to cheap drink made mischief!

In the 1840s a farmer Elliott of Havenstreet recounted that when a boy he was ploughing at the Nunwell estate when an idle gang of smugglers fired off their muskets, frightening the horses. A complaint was made to the owner of Nunwell who devised a plot to apprehend them. He invited the gang to supper and informed the press gang of the time his guests were due to arrive, resulting in them all being unceremoniously shipped off to a man o'war!

The darker side of smuggling

Daniel Boyce (sometimes known as David Boyes or Bryce) made a fortune of £40,000 from smuggling, but ended his life in about 1740 languishing in

Fleet prison. He built Appley House, a luxurious mansion near Ryde, which today forms part of the Benedictine Convent of St Cecilia. Together with his partner John Hatch he dealt in foreign wines, storing them in the cellars beneath the house. When caught and hauled before the courts Boyce avoided conviction by bribing witnesses and jurymen. Finally, repeated failure by the courts to nail him prompted a change in the law. Under the Ballotting Act of 1730 jurors were picked from a secret ballot box, and with the aid of this law Boyce was finally convicted.

Prison wasn't the only punishment for smuggling. Convicted smugglers could expect to be pressed into the navy, for conditions were harsh and few men volunteered. With the breadwinner gone there was often real hardship amongst their families. James Bucket of Brighstone was sentenced to five years on a man o' war but in consideration of his good conduct served four years and eight months. The hard drinking John Wheeler of Ventnor was also pressed into the navy for smuggling. While his ship was in South America he deserted and spent two years wandering the continent. He rejoined his ship at another port to finish his term, forfeiting all his wages as ropemaker and returning home after seven and a half years absence.

The threat of violence by smugglers resisting arrest and the carrying of arms by the preventive men and Revenue cutters inevitably meant there were deaths. Richard Matthews was caught one winter night in 1816 when landing at Sandown. Following his arrest, Matthews asked for his coat. Suspecting it might conceal a weapon, he was ordered not to touch it. He ignored the warning, and was shot in the head and killed. His body lies in St Helens graveyard, and his tombstone bears a warning in verse to the officer responsible to 'Prepare yourself to follow me'. In Binstead's Holy Cross cemetery lies Thomas Sivell, 'who was cruelly shot on board his sloop by some officers of the Customs of the Port of Portsmouth on the 15th June 1785'. Sivell was a ferryman mistaken for a smuggler.

Preventive men were at risk too. Officers could expect to be pelted with stones, beaten with staves or worse if outnumbered by determined smugglers. If the smugglers were armed they faced real danger; a pistol battle took place at Clamerkin Bridge when coastguards and preventive men surprised a band moving tubs of liquor from Newtown Creek. It is not surprising that some men employed in the Service augmented their wages with bribes or turned a blind eye rather than risk their lives.

In 1836 a Court of Enquiry accused Lieutenant Josiah Dornford and his

The gravestone of Thomas Sivell who was mistaken for a smuggler
and shot by Customs officers.

men of the Coastguard Service of 'collusion with smugglers, of accepting bribes from them, of falsifying reports' and other offences. Whatever the truth, so many islanders were involved in the trade it was impossible to make the charges stick. The court was swamped with an avalanche of testimonials on behalf of Lieutenant Dornford and a large number of prominent people appeared in court to lend support. He was found Not Guilty.

Informers, usually disaffected smugglers settling scores, risked their lives and could expect nothing but intimidation and abuse. When former smuggler and informer Thomas Mead joined the Customs Service he was set upon at Yarmouth by his old companions, who threatened to murder him. Cowes pilots told the captains and crews of incoming ships about Mead's infamy. Mead said, 'the few ships I have been boarded on the captains told me that everybody at West Cowes says I was an informer and ought to be hanged'. Two sailors came up to his house, one swearing 'by God, I will have a limb of him'. Mead and his long-suffering family were finally forced to leave the island.

William Arnold

In the mid-eighteenth century the Collector of Custom had twenty five officers under his control – searchers and waiters (officers who boarded incoming ships), a tide surveyor, tidesmen and boatmen and four riding officers. The riding officers had long stretches of coast to cover alone and the boatmen's job was equally hard and dangerous. They used oared boats, frequently rowing long distances in rough conditions, often at night. Their incentive was an entitlement to a share in any smuggled goods they captured. But they were no match for the bigger smuggling gangs.

In 1777 William Arnold was appointed Collector of Customs at Cowes. He was hard-working, honest and determined and soon observed that smuggling had increased to an alarming degree. 'Illicit trade is principally carried on in large armed cutters or luggers from two to three hundred tons burthen, with which the Revenue cruisers are not able to contend. It is not unusual thing for them to land their goods in open day under protection of their guns, sometimes in sight of Revenue cutters whom they will not suffer to come near or board them'. When offered more shore staff Arnold pressed instead for a fast cutter based at Cowes under his own supervision, and commanded by an officer he could trust.

William Arnold, Collector of Customs at Cowes 1778 – 1818,
fought a determined war against the smugglers.

When this was not forthcoming Arnold bought and fitted out the *Swan* from his own pocket. Under the contract system civilian boats could be placed under the control of the Collector in return for a share of seized goods. When it was wrecked he bought a second *Swan*, a 90-ton cutter armed with ten guns. Arnold could also rely on the naval cutter *Expedition* and a sloop-of-war, the *Orestes*.

As a result of these measures the smuggling gangs operating from the mainland became more wary, but among the local gangs trade remained brisk. In 1788 the Contract system was abolished and the *Swan II* was taken over by the Customs under Francis Sarmon of Cowes. From now on Customs commissioned their own cutters. When *Swan II* went aground in 1792 she was replaced by *Swan III*, again under Francis Sarmon. With the outbreak of war with France in 1793 *Swan III* turned privateer, preying on any enemy ship not under the protection of a convoy as well as maintaining its war against the smugglers. *Swan III* fell victim to French frigates and *Swan IV* to a French privateer with the loss of Sarmon, killed by a musket ball. *Swan V* went the same way.

Through Arnold's determination smuggling decreased. Over a period of 5 months in 1795 only 100 casks were landed between Bembridge and the Needles, due to 'the vigilence and exertions of the commanders of our Revenue cruisers'.

The smuggling gang

Local smuggling gangs usually ran cargoes between May and September when the absence of fishermen was not noticeable. But first the money had to be raised. Villagers would club together to finance a trip, often with a contribution from farmer, parson or squire. The shore gang would be alerted, which meant virtually every able-bodied man in the parish, all of whom were glad of the money. Farm labourers earning nine shillings a week could expect 3/6d a night for hauling tubs.

The chief traffic was in brandy from Barfleur or Cherbourg in oak 10-gallon tubs called ankers. Large profits were to be made by avoiding the duty on spirits, which was 32 shillings a gallon in 1825. Watering down added further to the profits, and many an anker was diluted by as much as 50% and colouring of burnt sugar added. It was then emptied into bladders and skins and sold to local publicans and the many illicit 'pop shops'. Women

A group of coastguards at Ventnor around 1860. Their job was to foil smugglers and protect shipwrecked goods from plunder. They were armed with muscket and bayonet, two pistols and a sword.

and children were often used; Sarah Neason was sent to Winchester jail for carrying two bladders of brandy in her basket. Eleven year old John Benzie spent six months there after six skins of brandy and four of gin were found hidden about him.

In the early days of smuggling runs could be landed almost openly, but as the government clamped down increasingly secretive ways had to be found of avoiding the Revenue cutters and riding officers. Yet smugglers had the advantage of an intimate knowledge of the island's coastline, many of them being fishermen by day. When chased they would shake off their pursuers by venturing where the Revenue cutters daren't follow. Dicky Dawes of Bembridge once gave them the slip by sailing through a narrow channel between two ledges. Even today Admiralty charts mark the ledges, which lay between Cole Rock and the Bembridge Ledge buoy, as Dicky Dawes Banks and the channel as Dicky Dawes Gut.

Smugglers resorted to hiding tubs in a false bottom to the boat or sinking tubs with stones off the shore to be hauled up later when it was safe. When ashore the tubs had to be hidden securely before distribution. Churchyard tombs were a favourite place, as were hidden cellars, caves, haystacks, barns, hedges and ditches. Fred Mew relates how a crop of tubs lay hidden in the furrows of a field for seven months. At the Back of the Wight the close knit communities were wary of strangers and even invented ghost stories to keep them away from landing spots. Despite the efforts of the Coastguards, smuggling didn't stop until duties were abolished or reduced, ending the large profits to be made.

Smugglers' half-anker tub and carboys.

COWES AND YACHTING

The Home of Racing

CHARLES II returned from Dutch exile with a gift from the Dutch East India Company, a 52 foot yacht, and the first yacht race took place on the Thames between the King and the Duke of York. By the 1750s yachting for pleasure was established on the Thames and during the next fifty years the practice grew among south coast towns, including Cowes, of holding regattas involving fishing smacks, pilot boats and Navy cutters. The establishment of the Royal Yacht Squadron at Cowes and its patronage by royalty turned Cowes by the end of the nineteenth century into the home of international yachting and the centre of a fashionable social world.

The Royal Yacht Squadron

In June 1815, shortly before the Battle of Waterloo, a group of gentlemen met at the Thatched House Tavern in London and agreed to form a club to share their common interest in salt-water yachting. It was called simply The Yacht Club and there were 42 original members. It brought together nearly all the owners of sea-going yachts in the Solent; only the Navy could rival it's fleet. The Prince Regent joined and when he became George IV the club gained approval to change its name to The Royal Yacht Club.

At first the club was primarily a social institution, though members' yachts took part in the annual regatta at Cowes, first staged in 1813, in which the boats sailed in a dignified procession around the Brambles or out to Stokes Bay. There had always been racing between individual yachts in heavily wagered private matches, but there was no formally organised racing until 1826, when, with the club now based at Cowes, a Gold Cup of a hundred sovereigns was presented to be contended for by members' vessels. Such was the success of that first race that the people of Cowes subscribed for two more cups to be fought over at a second regatta later that year. These early races were boisterous and keenly contested affairs with the crews sometimes

Lord Belfast's brig *Waterwitch*, built in 1832, exposed the deficiencies
of the navy's 'coffin' brigs.

coming to blows when yachts collided or became entangled – for there were
few rules.

In these early days many members' yachts still carried cannon for defence
against privateers and thought of themselves as an auxiliary naval fleet. In
the 1840s the club's vessels could muster 400 guns! The search for fast
designs had repercussions on naval architecture. Members' yachts were often
superior to many of the smaller ships of the navy. Lord Belfast took every
opportunity to demonstrate this and decided to build a 10-gun brig that
bettered the navy's latest design. The result was the *Waterwitch*, built in
1832. It would lie in wait for the navy's men o' war to leave Portsmouth then
comprehensively outsail them. This happened so often the navy eventually
bought her, forcing the then Superintendent of the School of Naval
Architecture at Portsmouth Dockyard to admit that 'the excellency of many
of the vessels belonging to the Royal Yacht Club . . . render the operations of
this distinguished club highly interesting and important'.

Lord Yarborough became the first Commodore of the Club in 1825 and he greatly encouraged yacht cruising. During the Napoleonic Wars private vessels rarely ventured far due to privateers operating in the Channel. But by the 1830s private yachts were increasingly cruising for pleasure in the Mediterranean and farther afield. To allow them to enter foreign ports without paying tonnage dues they were permitted to fly the White Ensign. Not all cruising members were as adventurous as Sir James Brooke. Aboard his schooner *Royalist* Brooke ended up in Sarawak putting down a rebellion. He was made Rajah of Sarawak and helped stamp out piracy and headhunting! Lord Yarborough himself was not averse to adventure; in 1827 he became involved in the Battle of Navarino, the *Falcon* being used as a dispatch vessel.

In 1851, the year of the Great Exhibition, Commodore Stevens of the New York Yacht Club brought the schooner *America* to Cowes to sail against the best in British yachting. A £100 Cup was put up for the winner in a race round the island. The *America* outsailed the competition and returned home across the Atlantic with the trophy now famous as the America's Cup.

The Squadron acquired West Cowes Castle in 1858 and for the next thirty years it remained predominantly a seagoing society involved in the improvement of seamanship and yacht design. Cruising was more popular

West Cowes Castle in 1858, the year it was acquired by the Royal Yacht Squadron.

than organised racing, and its members included many who were both colourful and adventurous. Ben Boyd owned vast tracts of land in Australia and was killed by natives in the Solomon Islands; Lord Dufferin sailed into the Arctic and wrote a bestseller describing his voyage; Sir Allen Young twice attempted the North West Passage; General Sterling, nicknamed Sinbad the Sailor, embarked on lengthy cruises governed by the amount of corned beef he could carry; J.J. Curling became a rural dean in Newfoundland and sailed up and down its coast tending to the spiritual needs of the settlers; Lord Brassey's *Sunbeam* was the first privately owned yacht to sail around the world.

The Prince of Wales joined the Squadron in 1863 and was voted Commodore in 1882. Under his patronage the social importance of the Royal Yacht Squadron was boosted, the cream of English society flocking to fashionable Cowes in the Prince's wake. As one complainant wrote, 'Cowes is no longer a half-civilised resort of rough sailormen; it is a Court. The whole of Cowes' life now turns upon the Prince of Wales'. The activities of the Prince and his fellow yachtsmen were closely followed in the press. The Squadron became increasingly exclusive and harder than ever to get into. The results of elections to become a member caused sensations in the social world, and neither noble birth, wealth nor the holding of high office of State could ensure membership.

As the prestige of the Royal Yacht Squadron grew, so Cowes Week became one of the principal events of the fashionable year. Of this social gathering, an anonymous observer wrote in 1887, 'the Castle was the centre and soul, the seat of all moral and intellectual life, and the spring of all its hopes, fears, plans, loves, tales and jealousies. And the centre and soul of the Castle was the lawn devoted to the wicker chairs and the ladies. It was the pleasantest of all pleasant places which in that happy week in August blossoms out with the fairest and finest women of two hemispheres; a distinction which gained for it the attractive title of the Deer Park. But the chief attraction on the Castle lawn is the Prince himself. The Prince appears, and a flutter ensues as the pretty ladies edge insensibly towards him for coveted notice. He disappears, and the flutter ends in a comparison of frocks and success of notice.'

In 1893 the Prince of Wales took delivery of a new and innovative yacht called the *Britannia* and so gave a much needed fillip to yacht racing. Three years later, not to be outdone, Edward's nephew, Kaiser Wilhelm of

The lawns of the Royal Yacht Squadron, known as the Deer Park, in about 1934.

Germany, built the great cutter *Meteor* to rival his uncle's yacht. They raced against each other for two seasons then the Prince abruptly sold *Britannia* (though he later bought her back) disgruntled no doubt by the pettiness and jealousies of his nephew. Edward remarked that Cowes week 'used to be a pleasant relaxation for me; since the Kaiser takes command it is a vexation'. On Edward's death *Britannia* passed to George V; when he died in 1936 she was scuttled off St Catherine's Deep.

After the First World War the old aristocracy, impoverished by death duties and taxation could no longer afford big yachts. The men who could were business magnates who found entry to the club barred by the old guard: Tommy Lipton the tea millionaire, Sir Howard Frank the estate agent, W.L. Stephenson chairman of Woolworths, Sir William Berry the press baron, T.B. Davis, ex-stevedore, and Mortimer Singer the sewing-machine manufacturer among others – none of whom were members of the RYS when they first became owners of large yachts. But wealth alone was not a passport for membership of the Squadron. Indeed, to be newly rich from 'trade' and own a large yacht were more often reasons for exclusion! Paradoxically brewers and whisky distillers were accepted, leading to this period being dubbed the 'Beerage and Peerage' era.

In an age when women were still without the vote, entry into the masculine world of the Squadron was inevitably denied. They were allowed onto the lawn to take tea and they could view the trophies and watch the fireworks from the Platform on the last day of the regatta if accompanied by a member. But they had to wear cardboard badges which soon became coveted emblems of social success. There was no Ladies room until the 1920s and ladies in trousers were banned until 1938. Even today, though women can join as associate members, there are restrictions on their use of the morning room and the library. The Squadron may have been snobbish and male dominated, even bordering on the monastic, but not all shared the attitude of one member who remarked, on hearing that the Countess of Cardigan had collapsed and died on the lawn, 'these damned women have no respect for the Squadron!'

Membership decisions were inconsistent, arbitrary and undemocratic. One prospective member was denied entry for being so presumptuous as to enclose his fee with his application form! Some people found such idiosyncracies infuriating. Americans thought the traditions and strict rules 'quaint'. To women the rules must have seemed 'sexist,' even 'misogynous'. Men like Tommy Lipton considered them petty and irrelevant. Even today, the Squadron remains a stuffy organisation and full of mystery; though if wealth is no guarantee of membership neither is lack of it a barrier.

The Royal Yacht Squadron did its bit in two World Wars. Members' steam yachts joined the Yacht Patrol in the First World War and one of them, the *Lorna*, sank a German U-boat, while many others were sunk by mines or submarines. In the Second World War the Castle was a D-Day HQ and many of the Squadron's yachtsmen participated in the Dunkirk evacuation. The Great War killed off yachting in the Grand Style but Big Class racing slowly revived as a result of George V's decision to fit out *Britannia* for the 1920 season. The Second War effectively finished off the Big Class and today it is dinghies and small keel-boat classes that proliferate in an era when yachting is more accessible than ever.

The America's Cup

The America's Cup is a 24 inch high solid silver Victorian ewer (wine server) made in 1848 by the Royal jeweller Garrards. Originally known as the 100 Guineas Cup (though it cost 100 sovereigns) it was purchased by the Marquis of Anglesey who presented it to the Royal Yacht Squadron as a racing trophy.

In 1851 rumours drifted across the Atlantic that the Americans were building a yacht to challenge the best of the English racing fleet. The result was the *America*, 'a rakish, piratical-looking boat' with a bluff bow, overhanging stern and raked back masts. It was intended to represent American industry's boat-building skills at the Great Exhibition. The principal owner of *America* was Commodore John Stevens of the New York Yacht Club, who was invited to stay at the Royal Yacht Squadron and compete for the Marquis' trophy in a round-the-island race open to all nations.

When *America* arrived in Cowes she was so fast she was thought to have a propeller, a rumour which the Americans fostered. The old Marquis of Anglesey remarked on seeing *America,* 'if she is right, then all of us are wrong'. On 22 August 1851 she beat all 14 British yachts and took the Cup across the Atlantic, the owners donating it to the New York Yacht Club in 1857 as a 'perpetual challenge cup for friendly competition between foreign countries'. At a time when Britain dominated world trade and its Navy ruled the waves, defeat by an American yacht came as a shock to British yachtsmen accustomed to supremacy. A determination to win back the 'auld mug' was built on a sense of hurt British pride that the upstart Americans could so comprehensively outclass them.

Prior to the Second World War Britain unsuccessfully challenged 14 times for the Cup – not always without incident or controversy. In 1885 the American designer E. Burgess was seen on the Isle of Wight studying the latest British yachts. So two years later James Bell's challenger *Thistle* was built in great secrecy and it was said that a false set of plans had been sent to America! Lord Dunraven challenged in 1893 and 1895 with *Valkyrie II* and *III* but his sour temper caused a bitter controversy, fuelled by his allegations that the American yacht *Defender* was carrying illegal ballast. Lord Dunraven was expelled from the New York Yacht Club, embittering relations with the Royal Yacht Squadron until in 1912 the carved eagle from the stern of *America* was found in a junk shop and sent as a gift to the NYYC to patch up the quarrel.

Tommy Lipton, known as the 'boating grocer', was a self-made millionaire, an ex-errand boy from the streets of Greenock who had no shoes and no place to sleep except beneath the counter of his master's shop. He challenged five times on his *Shamrocks* over a period of thirty years and was presented with a golden cup as the 'World's Best Loser'. But Lipton was shrewd, and his various challenges gave him free advertising, keeping his name on the front pages of newspapers here and in America, helping to sell his tea.

The most successful challenger was aviator Sir T.O.M. Sopwith who came close to winning in 1934 with *Endeavour*. A week before embarking for America the crew went on strike for more pay and were replaced by an amateur crew weakening her challenge. When Sopwith's protest during the third race was adjudged to have been made too late the *New York Journal* was prompted to write, 'Britannia rules the waves, but America waives the rules!' He tried and failed again in 1937 with *Endeavour II*.

In 1956 a rule change permitted challengers to be shipped instead of having to sail across the Atlantic. In 1970 the number of challengers was reduced to one. From then on an elimination series was to be run on the waters of the defending yacht club. In 1982 the challenger series were granted their own trophy, the Louis Vuitton Cup, the winner of the cup to challenge for the America's Cup

Finally, after 132 years, the sport's longest winning streak was broken and the Americans lost the Cup. In 1983 Alan Bond of the Royal Perth Yacht Club sailing *Australia II* beat Dennis Conner's *Liberty* in a close fought contest.

The Yachting Legacy

It is easy to see Cowes Week as a nine-day-wonder, all glitter and fizz but no substance. A brief break from routine during which the town comes alive and parties, only to return to a deep sleep when the guests are gone. Or does the influx of yachtsmen and women from all over the world bring a whirlwind of orders and create the momentum to carry Cowes through another year? Does the champagne event of the yachting scene, sandwiched between Goodwood and the 'Glorious Twelfth', put Cowes in the spotlight for the whole world to see? The truth lies somewhere in between.

During the Napoleonic Wars hundreds of ships waiting for a convoy would anchor in Cowes Roads and take on supplies and water while the yards churned out warships for the navy. After Waterloo the yards and suppliers faced a slump and it was fortuitious for Cowes that the budding sport of yachting and demand for pleasure yachts and yacht hands helped take up the slack. In a sense, yachting is a red herring, for Cowes has always been more than yachts. Over the years Cowes yards, especially on the east side of the river, have built paddle steamers, destroyers, flying boats and hovercraft. Heavy engineering was always more important than the building of elegant yachts.

What Cowes Week and yachting have done is keep alive a tradition of maritime craftsmanship that is evident in the many family businesses still thriving in the town. Pascall Atkey, founded in 1799, is believed to be the oldest yacht chandlery in the world. Benzies the jewellers was established in 1862 and has been awarded eight Royal Warrants. When Lord Louis Mountbatten was refused access to the Royal Yacht Squadron he would watch the sailing from the observation tower on top of Benzies. Chemist Alfred Beken moved to Cowes in 1888 to pursue his interest in marine photography and designed a camera capable of withstanding saltwater. Beken is now famous worldwide, with an archive of 250,000 images spanning over 100 years of maritime history.

Spencer Rigging have been responsible for restoring, fitting and rigging many of the world's most famous yachts, including the 'J' Class *Endeavour, Velsheda* and *Shamrock*. They rigged the radio masts for the pirate station Radio Caroline and in 1978/9 they fitted out the replica *Bounty*. Clare Lallows yard was founded in 1867 and acquired the reputation of building boats as elegant as Chippendale furniture. The yard made two *Morning Clouds* for Ted Heath, the ex-Tory Prime Minister.

No business epitomises tradition, craftsmanship and superior design more than sailmakers Ratsey and Lapthorn. Until the 1960s every British challenger for the America's Cup was equipped with their sails and from 1903 all American defenders wore their canvas. George Ratsey ran a coal business but in 1790 started making sails as a sideline. For many years coal was more important and his sailmakers often had to stop work to unload colliers. But sailmaking expanded rapidly when the Royal Yacht Squadron moved to Cowes. In 1882 Ratseys merged with James Lapthorn and 20 years later opened a loft in New York.

The sailmaking process started with the canvas, made from Egyptian cotton, being soaked and shrunk. In the 'spreading' loft the curves were plotted and canvas cut; in another loft 'striking up,' or preparing the sails for seaming, was done. Seaming was undertaken by skilled machinists then the sails went back to the 'spreading' loft for shaping and the marking of reefs.

Sail lofts at Ratsey and Lapthorns, Cowes.

The finishing of corners, making of eyelets and sewing on of ropes was done by hand. Ratseys made sails for the *Britannia*, her whole suit of sails using 4,000 yards of eighteen inch canvas. Her mainsail proved too big for the loft and a special platform had to be built across the road! Materials and technology have changed greatly since then, but Ratsey and Lapthorn survive.

THE DAILY BREAD

Earning a Living

Until the beginning of the nineteenth century the island's coast was a place of work rather than recreation. There was nothing to do there except marvel at the rugged and wild scenery. It was the preserve of fishermen in their secluded hamlets; the home of shipwrights, ropemakers and provisioners of ships in the north coast ports; the workplace of those in specialised industries like saltworks. The development of the seaside resort gradually turned the coast into a health and holiday destination, and a quarter of all island jobs are now dependent on the annual influx of visitors.

Salt for the Navy's pork

Salt-making by the evaporation of seawater was an important coastal industry from Saxon times. It's heyday was the seventeenth and eighteenth centuries when there were as many as 42 pans making salt, but the industry declined with the introduction of a salt tax and competition from cheaper mineral salt from Cheshire and Poland.

Salt production began in the summer. Seawater was bailed into shallow ponds called salterns at high tide and allowed to evaporate until a strong brine resulted. In the autumn the brine was boiled in large iron pans heated by coal-fired furnaces until salt crystals were produced. The salt was not only used locally but exported to London and was a lucrative trade.

Between Springvale and Seaview there was once a haven called Barnsley Creek. Around 1790 James Kirkpatrick, an island banker, had the creek dammed and the Duver embanked to create salterns. He scooped out collecting ponds, salt-pans and sluices, built a boiling house and housed his workers in Saltern Cottages, which date from 1640 and can still be seen today. The resulting product was called Bay Salt. It's main use was for salting pork destined for the navy, though some was sold in London where salt was dear. Until the early 1900s a heavy four-horse wagon, known as the salt wain, which at one time had made periodic trips to London from Barnsley saltern, could still be seen near Park Farm.

Newtown Creek has had saltworks since Norman times. In the seventeenth century seven saltworks were operating here, three surviving until about 1880. The salt produced was shipped from Newtown Quay. There were salterns too at Wootton Creek, owned by the monks of Quarr Abbey, on the western Yar near Saltern Woods and on the Medina River, but no trace remains.

Oystering

In 1784 the captain of a fishing smack, sailing down from Brading Quay, put his dredge down by chance and discovered an oyster bed that had lain there unknown for years. Other fishermen were naturally envious at his valuable catch but initially the captain refused to divulge its source. But crews of the Cowes oyster smacks were watching him like hawks, so when they each offered him a tub of oysters if he lead them to the grounds he accepted, with the result that an immense number of oysters were taken from Brading Haven.

Not surprisingly it was the Romans who introduced oysters to Britain and established beds in the Medina River, probably at Claybrook above Whippingham. A thousand years later the monks of Quarr were still farming oysters there and at Fishbourne. There was an oyster fishery at Newtown until a prolonged severe frost killed them in 1963. But the American clam came to the rescue of the industry by hitching a ride on ships crossing the Atlantic and finding a new home in the polluted waters of the Marchwood power station. They were collected and cleaned at Newtown and both clam and oyster were sold in London and Paris. There is no longer oystering at Newtown, the last company having gone bust.

Ships and Flying Boats

It is only fitting that an island people should have a long history of shipbuilding. In 1588, the year of the Spanish Armada, a ship of the line was launched for Queen Elizabeth at Cowes. Nye's shipyard began building ships for the navy in 1696 with *HMS Poole*, a 32-gun man o' war. Under Philemon Ewer's ownership the yard launched the biggest naval ship up to that time, the 70-gun *HMS Vanguard*. In 1802 Thomas White from Broadstairs bought the yard and brought with him a reputation for building fast craft such as revenue cutters. By the 1850s Whites had yards and workshops on both sides of the river employing 500 craftsmen.

Thomas White's sons John and Robert, together with Andrew Lamb, built the famous patented unsinkable Lamb & White lifeboats, originally for use on ships but later for shore-based lifesaving stations. In 1832 Whites built Lord Belfast's *Waterwitch,* designed to embarrass the navy over their poorly designed 12-gun 'coffin brigs'. The navy bought the *Waterwitch* and she was successful in capturing fast slavers off the west coast of Africa. A great variety of ships came down the slipways: small trading vessels and yachts, West and East Indiamen, naval brigs and clippers, large steam vessels for the Turkish navy and mail steamers for the P & O and Royal Mail lines.

Whites kept pace with changing technology as iron hulls replaced wood and steam replaced sail. They built torpedo boats and destroyers for the navy, paddleboats for work on the Niger, ferry boats, pleasure yachts and 134 lifeboats for the R.N.L.I. During the Great War Whites built 100 ships for the navy (27 of them destroyers) and 201 aircraft, and during the Second World War a further 26 destroyers and 285 miscellaneous small craft. When it closed in 1965 the shipyard, under both Nye's and White's ownership had the distinction of being the oldest shipyard on the Admiralty List, being represented for some 264 years.

Shipbuilding yards at East Cowes.

The Saunders' boat building business began on the Thames but moved to Cowes in 1901. They became renowned for lightweight, strong plywood hulls and produced fast boats such as *Maple Leaf IV*, a hydroplane which won the British International Trophy in 1912. As well as prestigious projects like Sir Malcolm Campbell's *Bluebird* Saunders had contracts with the R.N.L.I. to build lifeboats, but their long term future lay outside boatbuilding.

After a successful liaison with Tommy Sopwith to produce the award winning flying boat the 'Bat Boat' they concentrated on aircraft. Saunders teamed up with Sir Alliot Verdon-Roe, founder of the Avro aircraft company, to build flying boats of their own design, culminating in the doomed Princess flying boats. During the Second World War Saunders-Roe built Walrus and Sea Otter machines and repaired and re-equipped a variety of aircraft. In 1947 they designed the SRA.1 the first fighter flying boat, but it was never put into production. The experience of designers and workers went into development of Black Knight instead, a single stage liquid propellant rocket for the Blue Streak missile.

Saunders-Roe went back to sea craft when commissioned to build a prototype of the hovercraft that Christopher Cockerell had invented in 1953.

The hovercraft, brainchild of Sir Christopher Cockerell, brought crossing time on the Ryde to Portsmouth passage down to a mere ten minutes.

The result was the SRN.1 in 1959, the year that Westland Aircraft took over the company. The most popular production model, the SRN.6, has been used for surveying, anti-smuggling patrols, ferrying, fire-fighting and military purposes. The Columbine Works at East Cowes, constructed for the making of flying boats in 1935, became the home of BHC, the British Hovercraft Corporation, the world's largest manufacturer of hovercraft. BHC became a wholly owned subsidiary of Westland Aircraft in 1971, later GKN Aerospace, but now the Columbine shed, closed by GKN, turns out propellers for wind turbines.

Shifting Sands

In the early 1800s sand was being quarried from Hatherwood Point next door to Alum Bay and shipped to Runcorn in Cheshire, where it was used in the manufacture of plate glass. The white sand was being described by 1824 as 'the finest sand in the kingdom'. The material was brought round from Alum Bay in two local boats, the *George Henry* and the *Rose in June*, and stored in the Sand House on Yarmouth Quay. From there it was loaded onto coastal schooners which carried 200 tons each.

The sand was also used in the manufacture of porcelain and was taken by ship to the porcelain factories of London, Bristol and Worcester – even the West Indies. Between 1850 and 1855 a total of 21,984 tons of sand was shipped from Yarmouth. Following the Great Exhibition of 1851 the Cheshire manufacturers switched to better quality sand from a French firm, but sand was still being exported as late as 1908.

Alum Bay is more famous for it's coloured sands. They attracted the attention of travellers from the early eighteenth century and were mentioned in many guides. The turn of the nineteenth century saw increasing numbers of tourists coming by boat, by horse and cart and on foot to see the sands and scoop some of it from the cliffs as a souvenir. In 1839 Barber writes that, 'various ornaments for the mantelpiece are made from these coloured sands using phials and bottles' – similar souvenirs are still being sold in gift shops today.

Piracy and Privateering

In the unsettled times of Elizabeth I's reign the Channel was infested with freebooters preying on trading vessels. The distinction between pirate and privateer was a fine one. Privateers preyed on ships of the Queen's enemies often with the authority of the Queen or her agents; pirates plundered indiscriminately. Some of these ships were sailed by owner captains, like John Vaughan of Newport; others were run as a commercial enterprise by merchants like Henry Joliffe.

Cargoes from prize ships found a ready market on the island. Mead Hole, located on the north east coast between East Cowes and Wootton Creek, was the Elizabethan equivalent of a car boot sale where pirated goods could be horse traded. The place became notorious for felony, and stolen goods were referred to as 'Mead Hole goods'. In 1570 the Spanish ambassador reported to Phillip II: 'in a town on the island called Medol there is a great fair of spices, wines, wool, saffron, oil, soap, woad and a great number of other goods stolen from your Majesty's subjects and some French and Portugese.'

Shipowners and traders had two means of legal redress – an appeal to the Admiralty Court which was decided by the Vice-Admiral, or else to the Privy Council which was dealt with by the Captain of the Isle of Wight. Edward Horsey (Captain 1565-1583) and Sir George Carey (1583-1603) occupied both posts and thus could thwart or obstruct cases before them. Both men were involved in dealings with pirates and Carey funded his own privateering

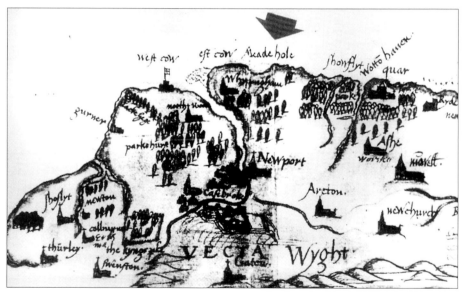

A sixteenth century map showing Meadhole, a notorious pirate anchorage between East Cowes and Wootton Creek.

Fishermen taking mackerel from a seine net in 1911.

operation in the Caribbean. Neither had much sympathy for aggrieved foreign ship owners. Peace with Spain saw the decline of piracy; there were more warships in home waters and greater inclination to use them to clear the Channel of brigands.

Harvesting the Sea

Any sheltered cove with access to a fresh water supply would have had a few families resident there scratching a living from fishing. Ventnor Cove had the Spencers, Wheelers Bay the Wheelers, Steephill Cove the Blakes, while Niton had Cottons, Haynes, Bastianis and more Wheelers. Each family had it's territory for potting, and the stretch of coast from Luccombe to Chale was renowned for crab, lobster and other shellfish.

Local withy beds provided material for pots, red withies being cut before Christmas and soaked in sea water to make them easy to work. The neck of the pot varied in size from 10 inches for crabs, smaller for lobsters. The pots were preserved with tar and lasted one or two years. Before being laid they were baited with conger, dogfish, skate or ray (and even rabbits, cormorants or stray dogs!) and 'stoned' to keep the pot upright on the bed.

Fishing was seasonal. Prawns were caught in February and March using pots baited with snails. Then came spring crab followed by summer lobster and mackerel, the latter caught using seine nets which were pulled ashore by a beach gang. Mullet and bass were also caught in summer whilst autumn saw the return of crab. November was for herrings and the winter for sprats using drift nets. It was a precarious living and in bad weather boats could be laid up for weeks. It was hard work too, for the boats had to be rowed or sailed. So fishing was supplemented by a little smuggling, salvage or farm work.

Chale Bay was famous for its mackerel, Niton for it's crab and Brading Haven was celebrated for it's winkles. 'Old church winkles' they were called and used to fetch the highest price of any at Billingsgate. A fisherman called Attrill used to load up his smack *Traveller* with winkles and sail up to Billingsgate, making as many as 17 trips a year.

The arrival of mackerel in Chale Bay was a great event, with old hands keeping a look out from early May. As soon as the shoals were spotted extra hands were sent for and soon there would be a flotilla of small boats with crews of five and shore gangs to help haul the nets. Gangs would come round from Sandown to help and there was keen rivalry to get the first catch to the Portsmouth market. The fish were sold locally to the cry of 'Chale Bay mackerel' whether caught there or elsewhere!

Most years see something unusual turn up around the coast. In 1842 a fin whale came ashore at Totland. It was auctioned at Gurnard and the skeleton saved and reconstructed (it can be seen today at Blackgang Chine Museum). Sun fish the size of dustbin lids appear regularly, though not all as big as the one gaffed off Bonchurch in 1841 that weighed 337lbs! In 1875 a basking shark was stranded at Shanklin that measured over 28 feet long.

When the holidaymakers began to arrive some of these fishing hamlets – Sandown, Shanklin and Ventnor – were transformed into seaside resorts. Fishermen became longshoremen working the beach for a living. They hired out bathing machines and rowing boats, beach huts and changing tents and later deckchairs. Some found themselves in possession of prime real estate and became quite wealthy. Most mixed these new occupations with a little fishing.

Victualling the Navy

St Helens was renowned as a safe anchorage. Shelter was provided by it's thickly wooded shores, and was much used by the navy and foreign ships in the seventeenth and eighteenth centuries. When the navy's ships left Portsmouth they generally assembled at Spithead and dropped down to St Helens Roads for drill instruction. In each new crew there were many landsmen – prisoners and pressed men – who needed whipping into shape in sail handling, gunnery etc. St Helens was good for fair weather drilling with the added advantage that if pressed men escaped they were stuck on an island.

In the days of sail it was not unusual for ships to wait two or three weeks for a fair wind to sail down Channel, and while delayed St Helens was a more comfortable anchorage than Spithead. With so many ships lying off the village, St Helens grew rapidly as a victualling depot, supplying beef, mutton, poultry, eggs, beer and especially sweet drinking water. Ships were often provisioned for round trips of eighteen months so fresh water was a luxury. For some reason the spring water of St Helens had miraculous keeping

Fresh beef for the Fleet at St Helens Roads. The navy brought business
but it also brought the press gang.

qualities, staying fresh on long voyages when other water went stagnant. Jermyn Richards had a brewhouse at Brading and grew rich by selling beer to the ships off St Helens. He bought Yaverland Manor from the profits of his trade.

If the presence of the navy brought advantages, it also brought the press gang. Fishermen were liable to be snatched from their boats or men taken in the fields, so next to the old Watch House was a cannon which the locals used to fire as a warning on hearing of the arrival of the press gang.

Cowes Roads was a busy rendezvous point and West Cowes grew as a victualling and supply port for ships gathered there. In 1627 Sir John Oglander reports seeing 300 ships off Cowes, among them many Dutch ships, huge East Indiamen readying for their voyages. In 1600 there were only four or five houses at Cowes but forty years on it was a growing town of 150 houses, bustling with activity. In 1641 the burgesses of Newport were

Cliffsmen collecting gulls' eggs at Culver Cliff.

so worried by the loss of trade from the growth of Cowes as a provisioning port that they petitioned the government, complaining of the growth of 'bakehouses, brewhouses, mercers shops and many other shops of trades and occupations to supply strangers with victual and all other necessaries.'

The Cliffsmen of Freshwater

Before legislation was passed to protect wildlife everything was considered fair game, and seabirds were safe on sheer cliffs from all but one predator – man. The cliffsmen of Freshwater would rob the seabirds' nests of their eggs or take the birds themselves for their meat and feathers. In Worsley's day 'a dozen birds generally yield a pound weight of soft feathers for which the merchants gave 8d; the carcasses are bought by fishermen at 6d a dozen for the purpose of baiting their crab pots'. Ethel Hargrove gives a vivid account of the trade in her *Wanderings in the Isle of Wight,* published in 1846.

'Neither fish nor fowl can haunt a coast, but the inhabitants find some means of turning them to advantage. Unable to get at the latter from below, the islanders reach them from above, by descending the perpendicular cliffs . . . They drive a large stake or iron bar into the top of the cliff; to this stake or bar, they fasten a strong rope, at the other end of which there is a stick put cross-wise, for the adventurer to sit upon, or support himself by; and with this simple apparatus he lets himself down the front of the horrid precipice.

'If his object is to secure eggs, he halloos as he descends, to scare the birds away; but when he wishes to obtain feathers, and the birds themselves, he goes to work in silence, and either catches them in their nests, or knocks them down with a stick as they fly out of their holes. The feathers of the birds are of value, and their flesh is used by the fishermen, who bait their crab pots with it. Some of the eggs are said to be very good eating.'

Dr William Bromfield in the introduction to his *Flora Vectensis* (1856), says, 'the eggs of different species of Larus (gull) . . . are forwarded by the cliffsmen to persons in London' and were also sold locally to visitors as curiosities. Bromfield also relates how lords of the manor used to farm out collectors' rights for an annual rent. Descending by rope was a hazardous practice; in 1808 an artillery soldier from the neighbouring barracks fell to his death while emulating the cliffsmen.

Birds' eggs weren't the only harvest of the cliffsmen. 'Half way down hangs one that gathers samphire, dreadful trade', wrote Shakespeare in *King*

Brading Harbour in 1840 before the land was drained.

Lear, referring to those who made a hazardous living collecting rock samphire from cliff faces. In Shakespeare's day samphire was a popular vegetable and was cooked like asparagus or used in pickles. Herbalists recommended the plant as an aid to digestion and to relieve kidney stones. In the nineteenth century rock samphire from the Isle of Wight was sent in casks of brine to London where wholesalers would pay up to four shillings a bushel for it.

Quays to the Past

The Isle of Wight has plenty of estuaries on its sheltered north side to provide simple landing places for the import and export of goods, many of which are now disused and forgotten. Until the breakwater was built between 1843 and 1847 Yarmouth was a natural harbour and navigable as far as Thorley by small trading vessels. Thorley pre-dates Yarmouth as a port by many centuries and its inland site gave it some protection from pirates. But the muddy estuary silted up and a landing place was needed nearer the sea, so in the twelfth century Yarmouth was laid out on the east side of the river.

Newtown is another medieval town built on the banks of the safest deep water harbour of the time. Called Francheville, or Newtown, it was an important port until silting up of the estuary and the increased size of shipping caused its decline. A visitation by the Black Death and the looting French in the fourteenth century hastened that decline. A short stretch of quay and a solitary storehouse are all that remain. Nearby Shalfleet quay was built in the seventeenth century and in latter years was used to import coal, accommodating vessels up to 500 tons. The stone building beside the quay is an old coal store.

Brading Haven was probably an important natural harbour in Roman times. On the banks of this considerable stretch of water rose the town of Brading with a quay to receive shipping. Brading thrived as a port for small vessels carrying coal and corn; there was a fishing community (Brading cockles and oysters were renowned); and, of course, there was plenty of smuggling. The quay was left high and dry when in 1878 Jabez Balfour completed construction of the embankment across the harbour.

Before the embankment was built between Seaview and Springvale there was a harbour at Barnsley Creek that reached as far as Pondwell House (now demolished). The harbour had a small quay to allow ships alongside the tidal mill. The ships brought corn and left with flour. St Helens tide mill took over the trade when the creek was turned over to salterns. Another creek with a tide mill was Wootton, the mill once standing by the Sloop Inn at the head of the creek. Over 100 years ago there were daily boats from the old Mill Quay to Portsmouth. Twice a week a barge, *The Silent*, brought corn to be ground from Southampton.

King's Quay between Wootton and Osborne Bay is a mystery. Some believe King John retired here to sulk following the signing of the Magna Carta. One old historian says he lead 'a solitarie lyfe among reivers (pirates) and fisherman'. Later historians doubt that King John ever stayed there though he did make a visit to the island. There is no explanation for the name King's Quay – and there is no quay either!

Ropeworks

Ropemaking was an essential part of the shipbuilding industry and at one time there were ropeworks in East and West Cowes and Seaview. Henry Bannister founded his ropeworks in about 1790 and moved to Mill Hilll

Road, Cowes, around 1820. Originally all ropes were hand made. The rope was twisted from several yarns by a man walking backwards manipulating a wheel and an apparatus of hooks.

Bannister's became one of the first British companies to automate the process using an American machine, Good's Automatic Spinner. The company was also the first to introduce wire rope as a substitute for hemp in the standing rigging of yachts. Known as Cowes Steam Hemp and Wire Rope Works, it was the most successful of the island's ropeworks, exporting its products to many parts of the world. It was taken over by J.S. White in 1956.

THE UNDERCLIFF

'The British Madeira'

THE UNDERCLIFF stretches for six miles from St Catherine's Point to Luccombe Bay and consists of an upper cliff of rock up to 70 metres high overlooking an area of irregular terraces up to 600 metres wide. The rock of the upper cliff sits on impermeable clay known as 'blue slipper'; lubricated by seeping groundwater large chunks of cliff have slumped forward to create the shelf of fallen ground and the broken and twisted landscape we see today.

During the last two hundred years there have been a number of major landslips. In 1799 Pitlands Farm at Niton fell into the sea and a hundred acres moved as if 'broken up by the action of an enormous plough'. At Luccombe two landslides in 1810 and 1818 carried away thirty and fifty acres respectively. In 1853 an overhanging rock was blasted for safety reasons and fell onto the old Undercliff Road which was diverted round it. The road was closed for good in 1928 when 120,000 tons of rock fell away.

The upper cliff is especially impressive around 'windy corner' at Gore Clff, where the well-defined striations of the chert beds look like layer upon layer of pancakes. Sheltered from the north by this wall of Greensand, and with its south-facing aspect, the Undercliff has a mild climate which has long been recognised as beneficial to health. From the early nineteenth century it attracted the wealthy, the celebrated and the illustrious to build villas and summer residences or make extended visits.

The Rich and the Famous

Bonchurch is tucked under the eastern end of the Undercliff and is where Charles Dickens stayed in 1849 when writing *David Copperfield*. The historian Lord Macaulay spent the summer of 1850 at Bonchurch working on the latter part of his *History of England*. He must have been under no pressure from his publisher to complete it, judging by his leisurely days: 'I rise before seven; breakfast at nine; write a page, ramble five or six hours through

Richard Worsley, Governor of the Isle of Wight 1780-82,
lived at Sea Cottage, Steephill in his later years.

copse wood with Plutarch in my hand; come home; write another page.'

The poet Algernon Swinburne grew up at East Dene and is buried in the new churchyard. Another resident of Bonchurch was Henry de Vere Stacpoole, whose novel *The Blue Lagoon* was reprinted 23 times in 12 years and has twice been made into a film. Elizabeth Sewell, the educationist and authoress, started a school here. Perhaps most remarkably, considering the air of middle class gentility associated with the Undercliff, Karl Marx stayed at No1 Boniface Gardens in the winters of 1881 and 1882 when recovering from a lung condition.

Sir Richard Worsley, who owned much of the Undercliff, lived at the now ruined family seat of Appuldurcombe House. He turned it into a museum for the display of the antiques, gems, paintings and statues collected on a tour of the Mediterranean and the Levant. In 1794 he built a marine villa at Steephill and moved there rather than live in a museum. The gardens of 'Sea Cottage' were adorned with three temples. Seven stepped terraces were planted with vines which vainly struggled against the salt air. On the lawns overlooking Battery Bay (now Sir Richard's Cove) shone six bronze cannon captured from a French privateer and said to be cast from the bells of Nantes Cathedral.

When Sir Richard died in 1805, Charles Anderson Pelham, later Lord Yarborough, who had married into the family, took over the Undercliff estate. Lord Yarborough was first Commodore of the Royal Yacht Squadron and a keen advocate of the cat-o-nine tails on board his yacht. His son built a house next door which was to become 'Lisle Combe' the most noted occupants of which were the poet and author Alfred Noyes and Admiral of the Fleet Sir Charles Madden, a brother-in-law of Admiral Lord Jellicoe.

On land bought from the Yarboroughs rose St Lawrence Hall, which was home to Jellicoe from 1924-35. Jellicoe was in overall command at the Battle of Jutland, an indecisive engagement celebrated by Germany as the victory of the Skaggerak. To a nation accustomed to naval supremacy it was an outcome which won him little praise, but he was made an earl and Governor of New Zealand.

At nearby Old Park lived William Spindler, a German millionaire, who was a great if misguided benefactor to St Lawrence. His scheme to build a harbour at Binnel Bay and a promenade to Ventnor was undermined by the sea's ferocity and nearly bankrupted Spindler, but provided much local employment. The remains of Spindler's folly can still be seen on the beach at Binnel Bay. He was more successful with his planting of over a million trees to curb erosion. In his native Berlin he co-founded a home for waifs and strays and a suburb, Spindlersfeld, was named after him.

Previous owners of Old Park included Sir John Cheape, a veteran of the Burmese Wars with 46 years Indian Service to his credit. Lieutenant Colonel George Arnold, a Gentleman of the Privy Chamber to King George III, moved from Northamptonshire in 1790 and built 'Mirables' as his retreat. Another soldier, General Sir Willoughby Gordon, retired to the 'Orchards' in 1817 after being invalided out of the army having served as Quartermaster General to the Duke of Wellington during the Peninsular War. The general's incompetence caused the army to be without rations for two days during a vital battle, and only his friendship with the Duke of York saved him from disgrace.

Successful manufacturers also bought grand properties. Those paragons of flour power the MacDougalls owned a fine villa and Twinings the tea family still do. Uffa Fox, sailor and marine architect, lived at Niton during the Second World War where he designed the parachuted airborne lifeboat.

The Orchards was once owned by Sir Willoughby Gordon,
Wellington's Quartermaster General during the Peninsular War.

In the mid-seventeenth century an orphan boy by the name of Thomas Hobson was apprenticed by the Bonchurch parish officers to a tailor at Niton. When the fleet appeared offshore one day he took a boat and rowed out to join up as ship's boy. In a battle with the French he climbed the mast of their flagship and took their colours. From then on he received the patronage of an Admiral and rose rapidly through the ranks. In 1672, aged thirty, he became a lieutenant, a captain in 1678, and Admiral in 1689. He was nicknamed by the sailors 'Admiral Snip'. He was knighted by Queen Anne and sat as MP for Newtown in three Parliaments. He returned to Niton to visit the old couple who had raised him. They had always thought he'd drowned and didn't believe who he was until he sang a song they'd taught him as a child.

'Almost Fairyland'

In 1770 Hans Stanley bought the Steephill estate, an area to the west of Ventnor which included a group of cottages and an inn at Flowers Brook. Half way between the downs and the shore he built 'The Cottage' as a retreat. Stanley was MP for Southampton from 1754-1780 and was made Governor of the Isle of Wight for life in 1774. He followed his father's example in 1780 by committing suicide, after which the estate passed through several hands before being bought by John Hamborough in 1828, whose intention it was to build a grand house.

He demolished 'The Cottage' and engaged James Sanderson as architect. Sanderson was famous for his restoration of Henry VII's Chapel in Westminster Abbey, but for Hamborough he designed a castellated gothic mansion, a fairyland fantasy of turrets and towers using locally quarried stone. In a cruel twist of fate Hamborough went blind before it was finished in 1835. Despite losing his sight, he still had the houses and inn at Flowers Brook demolished because they would ruin the view to the south, and

Steephill Castle, built by John Hamborough between 1833-5. When it was owned by the tobacco magnate, John Morgan Richards, it was at the centre of island social life.

rehoused the families in Ventnor. There were three miles of walks in the gardens around the mansion which were full of exotic trees and plants with fountains, lawns, bowers, an orangery and giant fig trees.

In 1887 Major Dudley Albert Hamborough left Steephill Castle for good after his son Lt Windsor Cecil Hamborough was killed while shooting on the moors in Scotland. Alfred Monson, a tutor engaged to help Windsor gain his commission, was accused but acquitted of his murder in what became known as the Ardlamont Mystery. The trial was one of the most publicised of Victorian times. Whilst in Hamborough hands Steephill Castle enjoyed a social importance only equalled by Queen Victoria's house at Osborne. The Queen and Prince Albert made several visits and William IV's widow Queen Adelaide wintered there in 1842. In 1874 Empress Elizabeth of Austria stayed for several months and the unfortunate widow of Napoleon III, the Empress Eugenie, also visited.

John Morgan Richards, the tobacco magnate, bought Steephill Castle in 1903 and continued the tradition of entertaining the rich and famous. Among his guests was fellow multi-millionaire John D. Rockefeller. Richards' daughter was Pearl Craigie, a novelist and pianist, who wrote under the pen-name 'John Oliver Hobbes'. She rented St Lawrence Lodge from Herr Spindler but after her suicide at the age of 38 her father bought the property, which survives as Craigie Lodge. John Morgan Richards was a keen supporter of a funicular linking the railway with the town below, a tunnel under the Solent and a 200 foot observation tower at Ventnor Park! His reminiscences are recorded in his book *Almost Fairyland*.

The Friendships Holiday Association bought the castle in 1930. 'Castle kids' occupied it during the war, children from Ventnor Senior Council School being moved there as it was regarded as a safer building against bombs than their school. From 1959 it remained empty and was pulled down in 1963 to make way for a housing estate.

'Crimson cough cottages'

In the nineteenth century tuberculosis was a real killer. One man who suffered was Dr Arthur Hill Hassall who was sent to Ventnor to convalesce. He recovered minus a lung and was so impressed by the beneficial effect of the mild climate of the Undercliff that he wrote to the *Lancet* in 1867 advocating the building of a hospital for tuberculosis patients in the Undercliff.

The Royal National Hospital for Consumption comprised eight blocks and a chapel
linked by an underground corridor and covering a quarter of a mile.

A committee was formed and land acquired at the western end of Steephill.
Funded by public subscription, the first block of the National Hospital for
Consumption was ready in November 1869 with accommodation for twelve
patients. Building continued for over thirty years until eleven blocks were
finished in a terrace stretching for a quarter of a mile. Each block was
connected by an underground corridor. Every patient had a single room with
a south-facing balcony, both of which were unusual as the infectious nature
of the disease was not generally recognised until 1887. As patients recovered
they were put to work gardening, though the sexes were separated and went
to different parts of the grounds. With room for 240 patients and 60 staff,
over 100,000 people received treatment during the 96 years the now Royal
National Hospital was open.

Treatment was simple – rest and good food in a healthy environment,
otherwise known as the sanatorium regime. Milk was served each morning
at eight followed by a cooked breakfast with coffee, cocoa, bread and butter.
Milk was served again at eleven then a cooked dinner of meat and vegetables
followed by a pudding. Tea was always tea, cocoa, bread and butter, and
supper was as ordered. Ale, port, wines and spirits were as ordered by the

Every patient had their own room with a south facing balcony.

Medical Officer. The average length of stay was 70 days and regimes varied in stages from absolute rest (in bed) to 'up all day'. Every patient had to rest between twelve and one and between five and six without talking.

The end of tuberculosis came with the use of antibiotics in the 1950s and this once splendid building became redundant. No economic use could be found for it and so it was demolished in 1969; the grounds became Ventnor Botanical Gardens while all trace of the buildings are buried beneath the tarmac car park. However the stained glass windows of the hospital chapel, designed by Ford Madox-Brown, William Morris, Edward Burne-Jones and Sir William Reynolds-Stephens of the Pre-Raphaelite Brotherhood, were rescued and installed in the parish church of St Lawrence.

SUGGESTED WALKS

When walking along the coast keep to public rights of way and follow the Country Code. It is advisable to get a weather forecast, wear appropriate clothing and footwear, and use a map. If you intend walking along the beach, especially beneath cliffs, be aware of what the tide is doing to avoid being cut off.

Fossil Hunting

PLEASE NOTE You should only search the loose material and report any finds to Dinosaur Isle Museum. Any fossils found in situ should be left and reported in order that they may be properly excavated. Novices would benefit from the organised field trips run by Dinosaur Isle, Martin Simpson and Dinosaur Farm Museum.

YAVERLAND. From Sandown take the B3395 towards Bembridge along the sea front and park at Yaverland Car Park opposite the Zoo. Walk east along the beach past Red Cliff and under the white chalk cliffs, returning the same way. Search the shingle as well as the cliff exposures. Best at low tide. Combine with a visit to Dinosaur Isle along Culver Parade.

WHALE CHINE. From Chale take the A3055 (Military Road) towards Freshwater and park at the large lay-by at Whale Chine. Walk down the steps to the beach. Walk eastwards towards Blackgang but be aware in summer of the naturists' beach. Return the same way. Alternatively walk westwards round Atherfield Point and climb to the clifftop at the next chine (Shepherd's). Return along the cliff path. Look in cliff exposures, shingle and rock ledges. Combine with visit to Fossil Shop, Blackgang and Dinosaur Farm Museum.

BROOK AND COMPTON BAYS. Park at either Shippards Chine Car Park (Compton) or Brook Bay Car Park along the A3055 (Military Road). Walk along the beach between the two over the ledges at Hanover Point (only possible at low tide) to see the petrified pine forest. Return the same way or along cliff path. Combine with a visit to Brighstone village to see the Village Museum.

Forts

FORT VICTORIA lies 1 mile west of Yarmouth off the A3054. Just follow the brown signs. A very short walk along the Coastal Footpath to Fort Albert and back. A

Countryside Ranger takes guided walks around the Park highlighting local and natural history. Other attractions include marine aquarium, sunken history exhibition, planetarium and model railway. Combine with a visit to Yarmouth Castle.

NEEDLES OLD BATTERY. West of Freshwater on the B3322. Park at Alum Bay 1 mile from Battery. Fort has a 200 foot tunnel leading to searchlight position and stunning views. There is usually an exhibition though theme may change.

YAVERLAND AND CULVER DOWN. Park at Yaverland Car Park on the B3395 road to Bembridge from Sandown. Granite fort is now the I.W. Zoo. Walk the coastal footpath to the top of Culver Down past old gun emplacements at Sandown Bay Holiday Park. On Culver Down is Bembridge Fort and old gun emplacements of Culver Battery.

ST HELEN'S FORT. Every year in late July or early August, during exceptionally low spring tides, there is an organised walk to the fort. Several hundred islanders and holidaymakers take part in the walk to the fort which ends with a barbacue.

Chine, Cliff and Creek

SHANKLIN & LUCCOMBE CHINES. Park on Shanklin Esplanade and walk along the beach (tide permitting) round the headland beneath Knock Cliff into Luccombe Bay. Climb the steps up through the chine (beware as they are often out of action due to land slippage) and return along the coastal footpath into Luccombe Road. At the end of the road is the entrance to Shanklin Chine which will return you to the Esplanade. Be aware of the tides and allow time to walk back along the beach if the steps are out of use. Good for rockpooling in Luccombe Bay.

CULVER CLIFF. Park in the far Car Park amongst the old gun emplacements and take the footpath to the beach at Whitecliff Bay. At low tide it is possible to traverse the wave cut platform at the base of the chalk cliff, round a small promontory known as the Anvil into a boulder strewn Horseshoe Cove. It is possible to view twin caves called the Nostrils a little further on. Return same way. Take the opportunity to go rockpooling off Bembridge Ledge at low tide.

THE MEDINA. Park at Cowes and follow the signs to the Cowes to Newport Cycleway. Walk or cycle to Newport and return the same way. Excellent for birdwatching.

NEWTOWN CREEK. Park in the village and walk across the wooden causeway to the harbour. Return the same way. From the village you can also walk along footpath CB13a then CB9 through Town Copse and along the sea wall to the public bird hide.

Return the same way or along the road.

Wreck and Rescue

THE 'PEPPERPOT' is a medieval lighthouse situated on top of St Catherine's Hill with magnificent views of the 'Back of the Wight'. Park in Blackgang viewpoint car park off the A3055 just outside Niton and follow the signs. To view St Catherine's Lighthouse from the cliff take the coastal footpath from the Car Park back towards Niton.

ST CATHERINE'S LIGHTHOUSE. For a closer view of the lighthouse park roadside in St Catherines Road off the A3055 from Niton towards Ventnor. Walk down Castlehaven Lane to Reeth Bay then along the coast to the lighthouse. Return same way or by the upper footpath leading back onto Castlehaven Lane.

BEMBRIDGE LIFEBOAT STATION. Take the B3395 from Sandown and at Steyne Cross continue straight ahead at the roundabout and next junction into Lane End to the Public Car Park on the seafront. Walk along the beach at low tide only to the Coastguard Look-out next to the Crab and Lobster. Views over the hazardous Bembridge Ledge. Return the same way or follow the Coastal Footpath signs. Combine with a visit to the Shipwreck Centre and Maritime Museum in the centre of Bembridge and a guided tour of Bembridge Lifeboat Station.

BLACKGANG. Park at Whale Chine and descend to the beach. Turn left and walk along to view the cliffs. Be aware of the tides and return the same way. Combine with a visit to Blackgang Chine where there is a museum housing a complete whale skeleton and an exhibition on wrecks.

Smuggling

VENTNOR. Park in the public Car Park called La Falaise at the west end of Ventnor Esplanade. Walk along the Coastal Footpath past Castle Cove and Steephill Cove to the old coastguard cottages at Woody Point. Stop off at the Botanical Gardens to visit the Smuggling Museum. Return the same way and combine with a visit to the Longshoreman's Museum on the Esplanade.

Literary Walks

BONCHURCH. Park on Ventnor seafront and walk to Bonchurch along the sea wall. At Monks Bay climb up past the old church and East Dene and return through the village to explore its literary connections. Keats, Swinburne, Dickens – even Karl Marx – have visited or stayed at Bonchurch. *Bonchurch A – Z* by John Goodwin is recommended as the ideal guide. Combine with a visit to the Heritage Museum, Ventnor.

TENNYSON DOWN. Walk the same turf that inspired the poet Tennyson to write some of his most famous poems. Park at Freshwater Bay Car Park and walk along Gate Lane towards Alum Bay to the Coastal Footpath by the public toilets. This follows the Tennyson Trail up over the downs to the Needles. Return by the lower path at the foot of the downs. For a short walk turn north at the Tennyson Monument, down through a chalk pit to the path at the base of the downs and return to Freshwater.

The Boat Trail at Cowes

The 4 mile Boat Trail is a heritage trail around Cowes and East Cowes. It takes about 3 hours including stops at points of interest. Signs have been sited on all 40 points of interest and strategic points in between. The signs are based on knots and signal flags. You can start in either town and join it at any point along the way. A leaflet with a map and the location of all points of interest is available free from Tourist Information Offices. Here are some of the things you may see:

EAST COWES

THE GRIDIRON SHED site was used to build boats for hundreds of years and the first seaplane was launched here in May 1913.

TRINITY HOUSE operates and services all lighthouses and bouyage.

COLUMBINE YARD is an example of British industrial architecture built by Saunders-Roe in 1935 for constructing flying boats.

CAVALIER PROPELLOR from *HMS Cavalier,* the navy's fastest ship for 27 years.

FALCON YARD was one of J.S.Whites most prolific shipbuilding yards.

HERITAGE CENTRE has archives, displays and local books for sale.

COWES

RATSEY & LAPTHORN arguably the greatest name in yacht sails.

CLARE LALLOW founded 1867 and famous for restoring classic boats.

PASCALL ATKEY founded 1799 and thought to be the world's oldest yacht chandlers.

BEKEN OF COWES world famous maritime photographers.

CUSTOMS HOUSE still in use as a Customs and Excise building.

SIR MAX AITKEN MUSEUM Sir Max was Chairman of *Express* newspapers 1968-77 and three times winner of the Round the Island Race. The museum has many fine items of yachting memorabilia.

The Undercliff

THE LANDSLIP. Park in Shanklin Old Village Car Park and walk past the Crab Inn towards the Chine. Continue into Luccombe Road and follow it past the houses and onto the Coastal Footpath. This winds through the area known as the Landslip. At Luccombe Chine take the steps to the beach (if open) to view the bay. Return the same way or continue on to Bonchurch. On the way climb the Devil's Chimney for a close look at the cliff.

COASTAL FOOTPATH. Park at Ventnor Botanical Gardens and cross the meadow at the western end of the gardens past the Childrens' Playground onto the Coastal Footpath at Orchard Bay. Follow as far as Woody Point where, tide permitting, you can descend to the beach. Return the same way. Ventnor Heritage Centre has a useful guide (price £1.00) with four walks in the Undercliff and interesting information on many of the houses. The Botanical Gardens has a small display of photographs on the Royal National Hospital for Consumption. There is much useful information about the Undercliff in the Coastal Visitors Centre in Dudley Road, Ventnor.

USEFUL ADDRESSES

DINOSAUR ISLE
Culver Parade, Sandown, I.W. PO36 8QA
01983 404344   www.dinosaurisle.com

DINOSAUR FARM MUSEUM
Military Road, Brighstone, I.W. PO30 4PG
01983 740844 or 07970 626456 www.dinosaur-farm.co.uk

THE FOSSIL SHOP
Blackgang Chine, I.W. PO38 2HN
01983 730233

NEEDLES OLD BATTERY
West High Down, Totland, PO39 0JH
01983 754772 or 0870 458 0022 www.nationaltrust.org.uk

FORT VICTORIA
Near Yarmouth, I.W. PO41 0RR
01983 760283. To book a guided tour telephone the Countryside Ranger on
760860

YARMOUTH CASTLE
01983 760678 www.english-heritage.org.uk

NEEDLES PLEASURE CRUISES LTD
Chilbolton, Weston Lane, Totland
01983 754477

COWES MARITIME MUSEUM
Beckford Road, Cowes
01983 823433 www.iwight.com

SHIPWRECK CENTRE & MARITIME MUSEUM
Bembridge, I.W. PO35 5SB
01983 872223/873125 www.isle-of-wight.uk.com/shipwrecks

THE MUSEUM OF SMUGGLING HISTORY
Botanic Garden, Ventnor, PO38 1UL
01983 853677

BRIGHSTONE VILLAGE MUSEUM
North St, Brighstone, PO30 4AX
01983 740689 www.nationaltrust.org.uk

HERITAGE MUSEUM
11 Spring Hill, Ventnor
01983 855407

LONGSHOREMAN'S MUSEUM
Esplanade, Ventnor
01983 853176

BEMBRIDGE LIFEBOAT STATION
Lane End, Bembridge
Hon Sec: 01983 873292 Boathouse: 01983 872201

COASTAL VISITORS CENTRE
Dudley Rd, Ventnor
01983 855400 www.coastalwight.gov.uk

MUSEUM OF ISLAND HISTORY
Guildhall, 136 High Street, Newport
01983 823336 www.iwight.com

SHANKLIN CHINE
Old Village, Shanklin
01983 866432   www.shanklinchine.co.uk

CLASSIC BOAT MUSEUM
Seaclose Wharf, Town Quay, Newport
01983 533493

THE SIR MAX AITKEN MUSEUM
83 High St, Cowes, I.W.
01983 295144

BLACKGANG CHINE
Nr. Ventnor, I.W. PO38 2HN
01983 730052 www.blackgangchine.com

FURTHER READING

Arnold-Foster, D., *At War with the Smugglers*

Blows, William T., *Reptiles on the Rocks* (1978)

Cheverton, Jim and Shepard, Bill, *Watching Birds in the Isle of Wight* (1987)

Dear, Ian, *The Royal Yacht Squadron 1815-1985*

Dowling, R.F.W., *Smuggling on Wight Island* (1978)

du Boulay, E., *Bembridge Past and Present* (1911)

Fraser, Oliver, *The Natural History of the Isle of Wight* (1990)

Heckstall-Smith, Anthony, *Sacred Cowes*

Hutchings, Richard J., *Smugglers of the Isle of Wight* (1973)

Hyland, Paul, *Wight: Biography of an Island* (1984)

Jones, J.D., *The Isle of Wight and the Armada* (1988)

Jones, Jack and Johanna, *The Isle of Wight, an Illustrated History* (1987)

Lane, Marian, *Piers of the Isle of Wight* (1996)

Mackett, John, *The Portsmouth – Ryde Passage* (1970)

Martill, David M. & Naish, Darren ed., *Dinosaurs of the Isle of Wight*

Medland, J.C., *Alum Bay and the Needles* (1995)

Medland, J.C., *Shipwrecks of the Wight* (1986)

Mew, Fred, *Back of the Wight* (1977)

Phillips, Ken, *Shipwrecks of the Isle of Wight* (1988)

Simpson, Martin, *Fossil Hunting on Dinosaur Island* (1998)

Venables, Rev E., *The Isle of Wight* (1860)

Williams, David L., *White's of Cowes*

Willis, Christopher J. & Roberts, Edward H., *The Lifeboats of Brighstone Bay* (1986)

Wilson, Lawrence, *Portrait of the Isle of Wight* (1965)

Winter, C.W.R., *The Enchanted Isle* (1990)

Witherby, C.T., *The Battle of Bonchurch* (1986)

INDEX